The Lazy Man's Way to Riches

by
JOE KARBO

TABLE OF CONTENTS

BOOK ONE

CHAPTER ONE

YOU'RE NOW ON YOUR WAY!

You are now on your way to having everything in the world you really want! Notice I say *"everything"* not *"anything."* There is an important difference!

If someone were to give you "anything" in the world for which you might wish, they would automatically *limit* their gift. And, they would be withholding far more than they were giving. "Anything" really means "any *one* thing." If the world were theirs to give, you'd get a tiny fraction of it and they'd keep the rest.

But, to have "everything" is a promise without limitation! And an important part of Dyna/Psyc practice is the need to detect and be free of *any limitation.* When you read the first sentence above, you may already have started to limit what this book can give you. It is important that you do not.

Let's look at that first sentence again!

"You are now on your way to having everything in the world you want!"

What was your reaction when you read it? Did you start to reject the *possibility* of truth in that simple statement? Did your habit-conditioned mind automatically say, "not me," "no way," "is he kidding?" The strong possibility that you did *just that* is the reason we're dwelling on it at length.

Only a fool would accept such a statement on absolute faith without any evidence whatsoever. But, a wise man, free of deadly self-limitation, would merely ask, "How?"

Don't be guilty of self-limitation. Don't reject the riches which can be yours by "knowing" or "fearing" you can't have them. Ask only, "How?"

How can you have everything in the world you really want? Go with me through these pages step-by-step and you will KNOW! Can you forget self-limitation for the moment? Can you cast aside failure-oriented doubt long enough to *try to learn how?*

That is all that is required of you at this step. You don't have to *believe* anything yet. But you must not *disbelieve* the possibility that Dyna/Psyc, **The Lazy Man's Way to Riches**, just might work for you.

What is Dyna/Psyc? It is the "code word" I have found most fitting to use when referring to that collection of natural laws or truths which make up this fantastic success formula. Dyna . . . because it is indeed a *dynamic* concept, one which moves you forward with great energy to the achievement of any goal. It is a source of great power, like some giant dynamo creating endless energy. And Psyc . . . because of two sciences fundamental to the method. *Psychology*, about which we have learned so much in the last seventy-five years, and those far less understood natural laws we are barely beginning to understand through *Psychic* Research.

> Dyna/Psyc: the programmed study and practice of achieving success by the planned application of important but little understood natural laws.

There may be certain fundamental truths in this approach to Dyna/Psyc which you have heard before. But now you will see even these familiar facts in a new light and you will learn how to *apply* them to your problems. You *knew* there were automobiles long before you were old enough or skilled enough to drive or repair them.

However, most of the things you will be learning will be new and perhaps even a little *strange* to you.

To help you rid yourself of disbelief, let me remind you of what Dyna/Psyc has done for me.

To put this in its proper perspective, you have to be aware of my situation 11 years ago.

I was out of a job. My wife and I and our eight children were renting a ramshackle house in a deteriorating neighborhood. We were driving an old Falcon we'd had to re-finance. We were $50,000 in debt. Under those circumstances, can you imagine how I felt when I was told that with Dyna/Psyc I could have "everything I really wanted"? I didn't believe it, but I had to admit that I had very little to lose. And maybe that's what saved me; I was desperate enough to try anything—even if it seemed foolish and ridiculously easy.

So they were saying that I could have "everything I really wanted" . . . well, I'd put it to the test. I'd set goals that were beyond my wildes dreams.

As God is my witness, these are the goals I wrote out during those black days—and this is what happened:

Goal: "I own a $75,000 house on the water."

Fact: Three years later I bought a home in a marina community fo

4

$75,700. With the improvements we added, it's now worth over $100,000. I know, because I turned down an offer for that much.

Goal: "I drive a brand new, black Thunderbird."
Fact: Within 30 days, I'd picked up an advertising account. It was a Ford agency. The manager said the Falcon I was driving was an embarrassment to the agency. He gave me a brand new, black Thunderbird to drive: a few months later I bought it.

Goal: "I earn $100,000 a year."
Fact: Last year I made twice that much.

Goal: "I own several small successful businesses. I leave the actual management to other capable people."
Fact: I do.

Goal: "I own a boat just like Steve Martin's."
Fact: For a couple of years, I'd admired a boat that belonged to a friend of ours. Within 30 days, he phoned and told me he'd decided to sell it for a fraction of what he'd paid for it—and I could pay for it any way I wanted. It was so spooky that I accepted his offer. Now we have two boats—and we paid cash for them.

Goal: "My bills are paid."
Fact: That was really a tough one to say without feeling like an idiot. But, contrary to my lawyer's advice (who thought I should declare bankruptcy) I had a meeting with my creditors. I told them that I wanted to pay them back, but I couldn't concentrate on the effort with the fear that they'd attach my bank account every time I made a few bucks. They agreed to a repayment program that I felt I could live with. I never missed a payment and a few years ago I paid off the balance in a lump sum.

Now, in case you are afraid the truths of Dyna/Psyc are somehow *personal* ones, producing rules that will work only for me, consider this:

Seven years ago I told a young man who sold me a boat dock about Dyna/Psyc. I did so because we had become friends, and he told me that the company he was working for was going broke and he'd be out of a job. His total assets were a half-interest in a $350 motorcycle. He owed $102 to the bank for a loan. He'd never earned more than $10,000 a year.

He dropped by my office the other day, showed me his original goals, and told me about his progress—every bit of which he credits to Dyna/Psyc. He reached and surpassed *every one* of his goals—and has set new ones.

Original goal: A salary of $18,000 a year.
Fact: He earns $40,000 a year and has stock options in the New York Stock Exchange listed company he works for.

Original goal: Ownership of a vacation hideaway.
Fact: He owns a half-interest in a $100,000 ranch.

Original goal: To quit drinking.
Fact: He did.

Original goal: To own income property.
Fact: He does. Two duplexes.

Original goal: To own speculative and growth stocks.
Fact: He does—$30,000 worth.

And there are lots of other people who have rebuilt their lives with the information I'm going to give you here.

There's a widow in Chicago who's earned $25,000 a year for the past 5 years, using my methods. The 70 year old woman who's traveled all over the world, making all the money she needs, doing only what I taught her. The man who works a lot harder than I'm willing to do, who, using these same principles, made 11 million dollars in 8 years.

Fact: *It's worked, without exception, for everyone who's tried it!* I'll admit, 'til now, I haven't shared the secret of Dyna/Psyc with too many people. Because most of the time, my only reward would be a patronizing smile. "After all," I can see them saying to themselves, "it couldn't be *that* easy."

But it is.

Perhaps you are wondering how so many people came to know of these natural laws and learned to take advantage of them.

As long ago as the 1950's, key executives of highly successful, really big corporations, began to be "turned-on" to the very same truths you are to receive. No one knows, or at least I have been unable to determine with accuracy, the names of the very first researchers into what might be called the Scientific Basis of Success. But, soon a number of costly but highly effective classes, seminars and private sessions were being carried on by the various practitioners.

The price for such services was high. But the thousands of dollars which were paid by the blue-chip executives was a paltry fee for the *immediate and spectacular success stories* which resulted from the application of the secrets they had learned.

Needless to say, as is always the secret with *power,* the men who were fortunate enough to have gained it were in no hurry to broadcast the news of it. They wanted to keep the powerful advantage they had received.

So great was the desire for secrecy that most of these power-sessions were carried on away from the executive towers of the corporate giants. Small groups journeyed to mountain or desert retreats for the closed meetings. The fees were so high that attendance was already limited to these top executives but, beyond that, only key people were even informed of the opportunity.

Since those early days, research has continued. The truths which evolved were the result of putting together facts from every phase of human development. And as the findings of this research were assembled, certain well-defined *patterns of power* making for *certain success* became evident.

Those patterns explain why "some must win, some must lose." But, more importantly, the rules evolved from those patterns eliminate losing for those who follow them.

Can you learn how to apply Dyna/Psyc to your life? Indeed you can. In the chapters that follow, you will learn things about yourself which you never knew til now! You are going to learn why you have not been more successful than you have (and, incidentally, learn why you did things which you later called yourself a fool for doing). And, just as importantly, you are going to learn how to have other people striving to give you what you want.

Never again will you look at a particularly successful person and sigh, "How lucky he is." Because you will know that "luck" or "fate" has absolutely nothing to do with success or failure. What we call "luck" is, in fact, a direct result of the correct or incorrect application of natural laws anyone can use effectively *if he knows how.*

Remember, the *power* to make things happen the way you want them to happen has always been available. You aren't going to have to *create* some new source of power within yourself. You are merely going to "plug-in" to the existing power.

The forces of Dyna/Psyc are very much like electricity. No man invented electricity. It existed in nature. But, until man learned how to make use of the already existing natural phenomon, he had no electric lights to turn night into day. Now *any* man can perform that miracle with the flick of a switch. He knows how to "plug in" to the electricity. You are going to learn to do this same thing with yet another natural power source.

But, just as electricity can serve man when handled properly and injure him if mishandled, the forces of Dyna/Psyc are raw power and can work for your good—or your ill—depending on how they are utilized. There is every chance that you will learn, as you study, that you have been *causing your own* failures through mis-use of powers you did not even know you had.

But, you have taken the important first step to undoing past mistakes and creating a whole new life for yourself—The Lazy Man's Way.

What represents success to you? Your answer would probably be similar to someone else's, but surely not identical. It should cover all the things which you feel make for success in your life . . . work, health, possession, love, for some tranquility, for others excitement. It isn't important how your view of success is different. But, scientific evaluation and research show us that it is important for *you* to know what you *really want out of life.*

Part of the work ahead of you will concern itself with an exact answer to that question of your desires. Why? Why do you have to have a specific inventory of what you want? Because surveys show that not two people out of a thousand know what they want from life or have definite plans for achieving their desires.

And the same surveys show that people who do have such plans are able to make life *pay off on their own terms.* (Why this is an important factor will be one of the things you'll learn, together with how to *effectively* create the plan.)

But a specific plan is only one of the factors in the success of truly successful people. Here's a list of some of the other things that come to mind when we think of a person's success. From the list, select what you feel is the other quality *all* real successes have in common.

1. Luck . . . the "breaks"
2. Family background
3. Social achievement
4. Basic intelligence
5. Education advantage
6. Good health
7. Enthusiasm
8. Winning personality

9.   Real determination
10.   Plenty of financing

Take time to examine the choices carefully before you turn to the next page!

You're wrong!

For the sake of helping you learn a *truth* which is essential to your acceptance of the natural laws that lie ahead, you've been tricked.

The correct answer, the other quality which all really successful people have in common, was not listed. Think of that for a moment. Doesn't the list include every factor we're accustomed to think of when we think of success? Isn't the essential quality there?

No. Many people have had combinations of the qualities listed above and have failed miserably. Yet, people suffering severe handicaps of bad luck, poor beginnings, little formal education, ill health, shyness, and only a "shoestring" on which to begin have been preeminently successful.

What is that second quality common to all really successful people? The second step after knowing what you want and having a concrete plan for getting it?

The ability to use effectively whatever asset you have!

Every successful person has *overcome his drawbacks* by making effective use of whatever time, energy, money, ideas, etc. he possessed. They knew it wasn't what you had that counted . . . but how effectively you used it.

A learned man once wrote that there were really only three kinds of failures:

Failure Type 1
Well-defined goals   —   Ineffective pursuit of them

This is the man who knows where he wants to go, but never quite gets there.

Failure Type 2
Pushes hard, uses every asset   —   No well-defined goals

This man is like a powerful ship . . . without a rudder. He always seems to be making great headway but never arrives.

Failure Type 3
Is the saddest of the lot. He has *neither* well-defined goals nor is he effective.

Whatever your pattern has been in the past, whatever has caused your drives for success to fall short of your desires . . . your answer lies within these pages.

Think of your position at this time as though you were the owner of a palatial ocean-going yacht. I am the Captain you have hired. The ship is yours, the choice of where you go is yours. My job is to first suggest the possible destinations and then, when you have made your choice, to lay out a course which will take you there. That course must steer clear of any hazard that might prevent our safe and speedy arrival.

And, since you will want to sail your own ship as soon as possible, we will see to it that you learn *everything you need to know* on this voyage. You will be your own captain long before we finish.

In other words, Dyna/Psyc promises you the assistance in selecting the *specific goals* which are a prime requisite for success and then shows you how you can achieve the *effectiveness* which will take you there.

What is expected of you? What must you do in order to make the transition to the successful person you *could* be? Very little—when you measure the reward against the effort required to attain it. That's why I call this the "Lazy Man's Way."

However, because so little is required of you, it does *not* follow that you can be lazy or haphazard in doing what is required. Quite the opposite. It is important that you *perform* in order to have all the benefits that Dyna/Psyc can bring you.

But, the tasks are not numerous or difficult. You have only to RSVP to this invitation to wealth, success and satisfaction!

RSVP: Read . . . Study . . . Visualize . . . Perform

As you go forward in the program, think of RSVP in these terms:

READ   I must *read* in order to learn the secrets which will make my life easier, my success in every field of endeavor certain. How else but by *reading* can I receive the truths which come from the natural laws expressed by Dyna/Psyc?

                But, if I *only* read, I cannot really *learn.* I did not learn my lessons in school by merely reading them in the same way that I read the daily paper.

Therefore, I must—

STUDY   I must *study* these things I read. I must do more than merely apply my eyes to the printed page. I must apply myself, mind, ideas, thoughts, to the substance of the words I read. By doing this I will begin to make the power of Dyna/Psyc grow within me. That power comes from understanding and to understand anything more than the simplest things, one must study.

                Once I am building that power, I will need to apply it to

11

my life situations. I will need clear outlines or blueprints of when, where, and how to apply the new-found power.

For this I will have to —

VISUALIZE   I must cultivate the capacity to *visualize,* in concrete form, everything I read and study. I must learn to take a mental or written suggestion and be able to *project* it like a motion picture on the hidden screen of my mind's eye. I must really *see* those suggestions, those plans, those goals, in *solid form* in my mind's eye. Then they can be mine, in fact, through Dyna/Psyc.

Visualization is far more than mere imagination. It is always more *complete,* more *detailed.* In short, it has the effect of adding the potential of *reality* to the unsatisfying dream that is imagination.

The man who creates a new and important invention often starts with mere imagination—a dream. But, as his mind ponders the idea, he begins to *visualize* with an ever-increasing exactness of detail. He begins to "see" his invention almost as though it were physically present in front of him. This I must do. It is not easy at first. But the unfolding of the program contained in these pages will provide *many ways* to help me *visualize—and turn dreams into reality.*

I can reach that plateau of ability if I —

PERFORM   The manner in which I perform is all outlined in great detail in the chapters which lie ahead. I have only to promise myself that I will try the outlined steps. The success factor is *already built into each step.*

This means the *scientific bases of achievement* have been studied and analyzed for me in order to create Dyna/Psyc.

I have only to perform the basic, simple steps outlined by reading, studying, visualizing and then performing.

When this R.S.V.P. is complete . . . success must be mine!

CHAPTER TWO

TODAY'S INADEQUATE YOU

A very wise man once said that there is a gift which all our true friends would *love* to give us, a gift which we probably *need* desperately, but a gift capable of utterly destroying even the deepest friendship. That gift is *criticism.* And, the more personal the criticism, the greater the sting it carries.

At the risk of endangering for the moment your sense of self-satisfaction, let me tell you something about your inadequacies. How do I know they are your inadequacies? Simply because you answered my ad, the odds are overwhelming that you suffer from the inadequacies outlined below. (But if it makes you feel any better, almost everybody does.) However, by responding to the ad, you also proved that you were willing to make some important changes in your life. You've already taken the most important step!

Now when I speak of inadequacies, I am not concerned with your size, weight, physical appearance, strength, manliness or femininity. The concern here is with the most important inadequacy from which any person can suffer . . . an *Inadequate Self Image.* For brevity I will refer to it as ISI.

This ISI is one of the first things formed in your life. It has a more *lasting* effect on your failure or success. It plays a more prominent role than *any other single factor.* This is true because it is the giant *controller* of your personal destiny.

If that seems hard to believe, let me ask you this: Would you like to try to face the daily tasks of your present world (job, friends, love-life, etc.) knowing and believing only what you knew and believed when you were *five or six years old?*

Think of the mess you could make of even the simplest tasks assigned to you, functioning as a grown person with the knowledge and beliefs of a tiny tot! Think of the impossibility of a mature relationship with others if your capacity to "get along" was that of a kindergartner!

Well, your ISI in all those areas that are important to us as adults was largely set in concrete by the time you were six years old! Challenging though that statement may seem to some, there is overwhelming scientific evidence to support it.

Once we have ascertained the point of woeful inadequacy at which ISI was established, surely you must wonder if it doesn't change as you get older. The answer (and we'll see why later) is "no," hardly ever, unless you deliberately set about to change it!

Your next question might be, what does this ISI control or affect? The answer: To a greater or lesser extent, *every single activity of the human being!* And it does this by placing a clamped-down, nailed-down, *ceiling on success!* It prevents the *adult* from ever reaching a potential beyond the concept of the *child*.

The direct result of this ISI is that the *average man uses about 10% of his potential!* And, it's no wonder. At the age of five or six few of us were convinced of our own great strength, power, abilities. We didn't feel very *effective*.

That feeling of ineffectuality was the result of the many pressures that were applied to us in those first few years. These pressures were the "do's and don'ts" of our early years as expressed in the *habits* we established. Scientifically these things are referred to as "conditioning."

Those pressures can be divided into two categories: Those which *help* us in later years and those which *hinder* our progress. The *helps* of those years was the conditioning we acquired which today lets us perform many of our daily tasks almost without thinking. In this group are included such diverse things as: tying your shoes; using a knife, fork and spoon; walking; talking; etc.

But what of the conditioning which hinders our effectiveness? Consider this example:

As a very little boy, Johnny goes out to the garage where his father is working in his woodshop. Fascinated, he watches as daddy is "making something." Soon, watching is not enough. He wants to "help." At this point two things may occur. One will result in a conditioning which will *help*, the other will *hinder* the self-image structure and the later life development as well.

If daddy gives him some safe but satisfying task of the utmost simplicity to perform, lets him do it; guides him to some small success, and then praises his efforts, the lad's self-image has received a tremendous *boost*. If this pattern of events is repeated again and again, confidence is built through the *habit of success* in this area of activity. It will *help* him build a better self-image.

If, on the other hand, daddy's time and/or patience is short, if the lad's interest and desire to participate results in only an irritating interference with the work at hand, no such helpful image-building results. The repeated efforts to participate (for little ones are not easily discouraged) may result in a final rejection by the father as he is banished from this fascinating scene—or punishment for what the father sees as deliberate disobedience.

Either way, the child has been taught a lesson. He has been "taught" or conditioned into a belief that he is "no good" at a certain kind of manly activity, or that he is "no good" merely because he has wanted to participate—"bad" because he was *ambitious*. His self-image has taken a blow, his *fear-factor* (of which we will talk later) has received a great boost!

To the same degree that this was an occurrence charged with *heavy emotionality* (loud voice, a physical punishment, lasted a long time), it will have a proportionately large and lasting effect on the self-image.

Few of us have been so fortunate as to have had only *helpful* ego-forming, or self-image, experiences in our early years. That is why today, it is a scientific evaluation that the *average person is working at only 10% of his potential!*

Where does that put you? Well, since you care enough about the future to buy a book like this, to read it, to TRY to improve your chances of success, you are already considerably *above average!* But, the fact that you are not already a smashing success means you are still not functioning *near* the maximum of your potential power.

Let's try to get an idea of your private view of yourself. Let's try to evaluate your *self-image*.

On a scale of zero representing absolute inadequacy, total worthlessness, and 100% representing as good as you could ever hope to be, check yourself in the areas listed. Take the time to think of each evaluation carefully. Examine the suggestions for evaluation on each chart. Try to be realistic and not mark yourself down because of emotional feelings or boost your score because of mere bravado. Only you will see the scores, and they can only help you to the extent that they are *realistic*.

Zone 1   The Ability to Make Money

	100%	You are earning all the money you could possibly use or want.
	90%	
	80%	
	70%	
YOUR	60%	
SCORE	50%	Earning the "average" income in your community.
_____%	40%	
	30%	
	20%	
	10%	
	0%	You are incapable of earning any money at all.

Zone 2   Getting Along with Others (not family)

	100%	You are universally loved, admired and respected by everyone you meet.
	90%	
	80%	
	70%	
YOUR	60%	
SCORE	50%	Looking about you, you are reasonably well liked, most of the people you know have just about the same number of
_____%	40%	friends, get along with others about the way you do.
	30%	
	20%	
	10%	
	0%	You can't get along with anybody for any length of time; nobody likes you.

Zone 3   Leadership

100%	Wherever you go, whatever you do, you are always the person others look to for leadership. If there's an election at work, in a club or group, you're picked to run things.
90%	
80%	
70%	
60%	
50%	About half the time you find yourself "guiding" or leading the way in group activities. The "gang" goes where *you* suggest for dinner, a movie, etc.
40%	
30%	
20%	
10%	
0%	You cannot remember a single time when others did something you suggested. You *never* get "your way" in a group activity.

YOUR

SCORE

_____%

Zone 4   Sport or Leisure Skills*

100%	At your favorite sport or hobby activity you perform at the professional level, good enough to compete with champions, without a handicap.
90%	
80%	
70%	
60%	
50%	You have reached that level of skill which represents the "average." Half the people you know are better than you in this regard, half do not do as well nor score as high.
40%	
30%	
20%	
10%	
0%	You never play well at any sport. Your hobby projects are total "flops."

YOUR

SCORE

_____%

*This may be an active sport (golf, handball, etc.), or some competition less active (chess, bridge, poker), or a non-competitive hobby (model building, painting, photography, sewing for pleasure, etc.)

Zone 5   **Family Relationships**

	100%	Your relationship with your family group is so outstanding that you might be selected by some civic group as the "best of the year."
	90%	
	80%	
	70%	You get along better with your family than *most* of the people you know. Less friction, fights . . . more shared pleasure.
YOUR	60%	
SCORE	50%	Looking around you, you get along with your family no better and yet no worse than all the rest of the world.
_____%	40%	
	30%	
	20%	
	10%	
	0%	You are totally unable to get along with your family.

Zone 6   **Your Work Skills***

	100%	You are better at your job than anyone else you know or have ever heard about. You're great!
	90%	
	80%	
	70%	
YOUR	60%	
SCORE	50%	You are no better and no worse than most of the other people you know doing the same job.
_____%	40%	
	30%	
	20%	
	10%	
	0%	You are so bad at your job you shouldn't even be paid for doing it.

*If you intensely dislike the work you are doing, give yourself an extra 10 points if you are rating yourself at better than 50%. People who do work they despise at a better than average work-level tend to penalize themselves here.

Zone 7		**Your Powers of Persuasion**

	100%	You could sell an electric fan to an eskimo. You could talk a miser into giving you his life's savings. You could convince a dyed-in-the-wool politician to vote for the opposition candidate.
	90%	
	80%	
	70%	
YOUR	60%	
SCORE	50%	You are not especially persuasive when you try to convince others *but* you are no worse at this than most of the other people you know.
_____%	40%	
	30%	
	20%	
	10%	
	0%	You cannot remember ever having talked anyone into doing anything they didn't originally want to do.

Zone 8		**How Lucky are You?**

	100%	You are *always* a winner. Door prizes, raffles or drawings seem to be designed with you in mind. Lady Luck is your buddy.
	90%	
	80%	
	70%	You may lose the *little* breaks, but the *big things* come your way.
YOUR	60%	
SCORE	50%	Looking around you, you would have to admit you experience "good luck" in life just about as often as anybody else. You get as many "breaks" as most people get.
_____%	40%	
	30%	
	20%	
	10%	
	0%	If there is a way for something to go wrong . . . it will go wrong for you. You seem to have been born under an unlucky star.

Zone 9   How "Smart" are You?

NOTE! We are not speaking of education, things you learned or failed to learn in school. Nor are we speaking of how well you know how to do your work. "Smart" here means the natural ability to "catch on fast," figure things out for yourself, evaluate a situation for yourself and know the "best" thing to do.

	100%	They haven't made the man who can fool you.
	90%	
	80%	
	70%	
YOUR	60%	
SCORE	50%	No "smarter" nor "dumber" than most everybody else.
_____%	40%	
	30%	
	20%	
	10%	
	0%	This can't be you—you wouldn't have been smart enough to investigate the possibility of this book.

Zone 10   How do Others See You?

	100%	It is clear that everyone you know sees you as their superior. They cannot help but "look up" to you in every way.
	90%	
	80%	
	70%	
YOUR	60%	
SCORE	50%	Your "image" in other people's eyes is probably no better and yet no worse than the average.
_____%	40%	
	30%	
	20%	
	10%	
	0%	You are convinced that everyone looks down on you, feels you are "beneath" them in every important way.

THE END

Now, go back and total all the ten scores you have given yourself. Then divide that total by 10.

Zone 1 _____

Zone 2 _____

Zone 3 _____

Zone 4 _____

Zone 5 _____

Zone 6 _____

Zone 7 _____

Zone 8 _____

Zone 9 _____

Zone 10 _____

Total _____ ÷ 10 = _____

This is your composite Self-Image Rating

The significance of this rating is even greater if you will now take the scores from just three zones of the test — Zones 1, 2, and 8. Enter them in the spaces provided below on the left and divide by 3. Then write your composite (which you calculated earlier) in the space on the right.

Zone 1 _____   Score from before

Zone 2 _____   (composite rating)

Zone 8 _____   for comparison:

Total _____

÷ 3 = _____   _____

The 1-2-8 scores, which we have averaged on the left above, are what we might call **How Things Are** scores. They relate to what is and is not *happening* for you. They are an *evaluation of current success.*

How do they compare with your self-image evaluation from all zones as entered at the right above?

Are you as successful as even *you* think you deserve to be? Is the right hand score higher than the left? If not, then you are not even achieving what you *know* you should. And, I must assure you, that right hand score is undoubtedly lower than it should be!

SUMMARY

1. Most everyone has an inadequate self-image (ISI), *except* those people who are outstandingly successful.

2. Freeing yourself of an ISI makes for success.

3. The success you have now is probably *less* than even your ISI should lead you to expect.

4. Dyna/Psyc is going to change your self-image, which will in turn change your degree of success. *Both* will be moving up from this moment on!

Save the scores you have calculated and, ninety days from today, test yourself again and see what a dramatic difference your application of the natural power of Dyna/Psyc has made. I promise you that you will be amazed.

CHAPTER THREE

FEAR AS A FACTOR

Although few people ever realize it, *fear* plays an overwhelmingly important role in the early-child conditioning. And, since we have that early conditioning to thank for our later ISI, it is important that we understand two unique qualities of fear as a conditioning factor.

1.   Fear is always a "hindering" force.
2.   Fear is generally a "buried" force.

Let me illustrate those two qualities by two specific examples of fear-conditioning.

Praise for a job well done, as in the case of the wise father with the child who wants to participate in the workshop project, is a "helping" force. It is positive in nature. It is a happily remembered experience. Praise is something to be sought after; we want to repeat the pleasure of the feeling of being praised so we try again and again to do something that earns more praise.

But what of the other side of the coin—the *rejection* or *punishment* unwisely meted out? It is designed to be and operates as a "hindering force." It is negative in nature. It creates fear. It creates fear of the painful experience being repeated. And, since it is unpleasant to remember, it is shut out of the conscious mind as soon as possible. Notice I said the "conscious" mind, for, with the *strong* impact of fear, it is *not lost entirely*. It plays its conditioning role long after the conscious rememberance is gone. It is suppressed and slips down into the subconscious mind.

So, we have fear, which *hinders* us in years to come, but which is *hidden* from our conscious thoughts.

To observe this in action, let us assume that some years after the child had been rewarded or reprimanded (perhaps on several occasions) in the manner outlined, a new situation arises.

Father calls son and announces the time has come to "learn how to handle tools." Father anticipates great joy on the part of son at this announcement. He is looking forward to the fun he and son will have working together in the woodshop. But such will not be the case.

Son does not *remember* the things that happened so long ago when he was so young, but, he *feels very uneasy*. Son has been conditioned to *fear* the wood-working, or anything in connection with it. Is it surprising that the son probably won't be very excited about the idea, will have trouble trying to do what his father asks, will be prone to fail when he tries (thus releasing him from having to continue)?

Some prime examples of the kind of *deliberate* remarks that become conditioning for the very young carry in their own terms the fear-factor they will create.

"You're stupid."

"You never do anything right."

"You're always so clumsy."

"You'll never learn anything."

"You'll never be as (smart, nice, good, etc.) as your (brother-sister)."

"I know you're always lying . . . I'll never believe you."

When we add to this the number of unintentional conditionings that come about accidentally (through spilling things, breaking objects, saying the wrong thing, various other childhood mistakes) it is not surprising that many, many fears of failure have found a permanent home deep in our subconscious minds. All these fears help shape our view of ourselves. And so fear is largely responsible for our Inadequate Self Image (ISI).

Why is the conditioning of the early years so effective in shaping today's image and even activities of an adult? Because the subconscious levels of the mind, while powerful, are *non-critical*. What is fed into them is all accepted as fact without any regard to *logic or later learning*.

To alter conditioning of this sort, we must bring new conditioning to bear. It does not matter that we know *today* that a failure at the age of four does not decree similar failures as an adult. The conscious mind uses logic, the unconscious does not.

The best way to understand this is to think of dreams you have had in the past in which impossibilities seemed quite reasonable while you were asleep. "I was flying through space," "I was in this house . . . but it became a boat," "I fell off the cliff but I just floated to the ground." None of these things seem unreasonable while we are sleeping, but awake we would recognize them immediately as impossibilities.

They are accepted while asleep because the lower level of consciousness *has no critical judgment or logic*. This means that all those fears we have suppressed to the below-consciousness level stay there *unchallenged by reality* as we have grown and matured in our conscious minds.

The fears and repressed impressions of your childhood years, based on the most childish lack of understanding often rule your activities today!

I will give you *new conditioning* thru Dyna/Psyc to replace that faulty *old* conditioning that is blocking your way to success.

That conditioning will permit you to both *be* a more adequate person and also to *see* yourself as more adequate. These two things accomplished, you will be a success!

For, realizing to the maximum your *true* potential, instead of limiting yourself to the ISI view of your potential, will make all the difference in the world. You will see tangible proof of this when, ninety days from now, you test yourself again with the material we have already presented.

CHAPTER FOUR

WE BEGIN

You and I have now examined together some important concepts which you must have before we commence the actual work of improvement. We are now ready for your first positive action.

It is an action which sounds easy. But don't be fooled; it is going to take you quite a time to complete. And I promise you it is going to produce some truths about yourself that you *never really* knew until now.

Your first positive action is to answer this short question:

"What do you want?"

The work of it begins when I tell you that you must answer that question *fully and completely in black and white!* Right now you must begin a complete *list* of what you want.

Why such a detailed list? Because that is the first step to getting them! This list becomes a list of your *goals*, your *destinations!*

Tell me this. Can you imagine a man going to the nearest airport to catch a plane with only the *vaguest idea* of where he wanted to go? If you were the ticket seller, what would you do to help him? Can you visualize what would happen?

Man:	I'd like a ticket, please.
You:	Certainly, sir, where to?
Man:	Oh . . . uh . . . someplace nice.
You:	I don't understand.
Man:	Well, it's important I "get someplace." I don't want to just waste time. I want to really get someplace.
You:	Someplace like . . . where?
Man:	Oh, someplace where I can be happy. Where I can have a good income. Get a new car, maybe. Perhaps become an executive with a good company or even have my own business of some sort. Be able to take good care of my wife and kids. You know, I'd like to get someplace where things were really great for me and my family. Just give me a ticket, I'll pay for it.

You: But, sir, I can't sell you a ticket until you know *exactly where you want to go.*

Wouldn't that be your reaction? You would have no way to help that man until he could tell you where he wanted to go.

And, isn't that what you've been saying to life? "I want to get someplace" covers everything and yet nothing! One thinks he has a goal because he wants to "be somebody." But, until there is a very clear picture of that position, he cannot hope to achieve it.

Looking at your life in this way, it isn't surprising that you have not already reached the height of success you might desire . . . on the contrary, it is *remarkable* that you have achieved any success at all. Without clear, well defined goals, success is impossible.

We are now going to establish those goals. But we are going to put them first into the simplest practical terms. We will be exact, for simplicity requires exactness.

To make it easy for you to list your wants, we have set up several categories and a few typical suggestions to illustrate what "want" fits each category. Go through the following, making a list of all the things you want.

Things I Need RIGHT NOW!

If I were to meet you in person at this moment and, taking out my checkbook, offered to take care of anything for which you had an immediate need, this is the list you would hand me:

Suggestions: I Need:

New Furniture   _____

Car repair   _____

Bills paid   _____

Medical insurance   _____

New suit   _____

Operation   _____

Dental work   _____

Rent or mortgage payment   _____

A new washing machine   _____

An air-conditioner   _____

or	_____
anything necessary to	_____
satisfy your current	_____
requirements	_____

Note: Don't be afraid to put *everything* you need on your list. Don't start off thinking in a "limited" manner. Put it all down.

That list complete, we move to list number two. It is not a list of things you *need*, but a list of things you *want* to have, need them or not. And, the sky's the limit. Anything you want, now or sometime in the future.

Things I Want:

Suggestions:	I Want:
Rolls Royce	_____
$100,000 house	_____
50-foot yacht	_____
An original Renoir	_____
One year trip around	_____
the world	_____
$500,000 in the bank	_____

_____
_____
_____

Now, if you consider it for a moment, it is clear that you want more out of life than just *things*. Mere possessions do not represent the sum total of what we need to enjoy full, successful lives.

Besides possessing *things*, we need certain *qualities* or *attributes* of personality and character. These intangible characteristics are needed for many reasons. To protect the possessions we might have, to guarantee our continued success, to have the respect, friendship, trust or whatever other feelings we want from others.

Our picture of success, therefore, has another list that must be made before we can establish our goals with certainty, the personal qualities you want.

The Personal Qualities I Need and Want:

Suggestions:	I Need or Want:
Ability to concentrate	_____
Real personal confidence	_____
Power to stop "putting off" things	_____
To be more aggressive	_____
Ability to finish what I start	_____
More original thinking- creativity	_____
To have a better disposition	_____
To stop "wasting time"	_____
To be friendlier to others	_____
To be a leader	_____
To be in good health	_____
To be enthusiastic	_____

_____

_____

_____

_____

_____

_____

_____

_____

_____

_____

_____

CHAPTER FIVE

TURNING "LISTS" INTO GOALS

Now you have completed the first step in arriving at the blueprint for the future—which is the prime requisite to using Dyna/Psyc to attain riches. You have made lists of those things, tangible and intangible, which make up your desires.

The next step is laying out those *listed* items in a manner that lends itself to the constant "use" which your success will require. In short, we must turn loose "lists" into concrete goals. This must be done by applying to the lists certain *qualities* or *points of reference* in order to make them entirely consistent with you, your life, and with each other.

Below is a check list for goal development; take each one of the needs and desires you have listed and examine it carefully. The wish may have to be altered slightly to meet all the tests below, but it can be. Once the wish is in a form which will meet each test below . . . *write it down*. These writings are your GOALS.

Remember, this is one of the most important steps in your progress; if you do not write your goals, you cannot use them as set forth in later chapters. If they are not made to conform to the check list below, you will find you cannot use them properly and they are far less effective.

Start writing *after* checking. And do it now!

1. Do you *really* want this?
   (Or will it just "sound good" if someone else reads it? . . . or is it so small a goal you think you have a good chance of getting it? This must be something you *really* want—the ultimate!)
2. Does this goal *contradict* any other goal I am setting?
   (i.e.: wanting a $250,000 house with a $20,000/year income?)
   Solution: raise your salary or income goal.
3. Any problems with goal cooperation?
   (Would your family be against your achieving them? Talk it over and adjust them.)

4. Is it positive rather than negative?
   (As we said before—what you want, not what you want to get *rid* of.)
5. Is it expressed in *total* detail?
   (Not a big new car; not a big, new $15,000 car; not a big, fancy Mercedes; instead: a brand new, black Mercedes, Model 350SL with _____ listing every detail as though you had to depend on this description alone after giving the company your cash!) . . . or anything else: (if it's a house, make it exact in the same degree of detail.)
6. Is it realistic?
   (And here I only mean: is it possible for some human being to achieve it? I do *not* mean is it realistic for the *you* of today to have it. The realism to which I have reference is shown by:
   Unrealistic: I want to fly through the air without a plane or any other appliance of flight.
   Realistic: I want to pilot my own private $750,000 jet aircraft.
   If it's a goal *someone* could attain, it's a realistic enough goal.)
7. Is this goal high enough?
   (Because this factor is so important, and so often misunderstood, I want to tell you about it before we go any further.)
   Number seven is the most serious checkpoint for turning your lists into goals, because it is the last chance I have to persuade you to *stop limiting yourself.*
   If you have asked for an income (a paltry two or three thousand dollars more than what you are making), if you've asked for a position which is only up the ladder a rung or two from where you now stand . . . you are asking not to succeed!
   More than that, you are guaranteeing you will not succeed! You're using what should be a FLOOR for a CEILING! Don't use the goal method as a system of *limitation.*
   Reach out! Set the goal limit in any area of your life at the very peak of what you'd like to have—*not* at what you think doesn't sound too "greedy" or "unreal."
   Be sure your goals are set high enough! I cannot emphasize this too much. There is no goal which is so high that it is not realistic if some human being can make or has made it! (Take a look at number six on our check list again.)
   Nothing should enter your mind at this point in time as to how you are going to achieve these goals!
   That's not your problem; that's *my* problem. I've made you a promise . . . "anything in the world you really want." All I'm asking

you to do now is make up a full and complete list; not to decide for yourself whether or not you could achieve a certain goal.

I'll show you the "how you get" . . . after you've established the "what you want."

8. Am I including the personality factors necessary to goal achievement? (If you are going to have changed circumstances, you will need the perseverance, self-confidence, etc., which you know are requisites. Don't worry about how to get the newer and better qualities any more than you worried about the "things" which are your goals. Just *list* them with the other goals.)

9. Is each goal stated as though already accomplished?

(That is . . . are the things you *want* worded on the goal list as though you *already had* them? They must be!

Don't write: "I want . . . I wish . . . I need."

Do write: "I have . . . I am . . . I own."

Examples:

I own a brand new, black Mercedes automobile, Model 350SL, equipped with . . . etc., etc.

I am an effective person who always follows through on things I start . . . etc.

Note: This form is essential to the psychological and psychic effectiveness of the declarations which are to come. Be certain you use this form in writing up your goals.

That is the check-list. Now there is nothing in the way of your writing your goals except one thing . . . procrastination!

In order to begin now to defeat that enemy of your success to come, there is but one thing to do . . . right now, *start writing your goals!*

What Comes First?

In addition to the goals you have listed as needs and wants and now are converting to positive goals, there are a few which I ask that you include on your list.

I ask that you include them because it has been my experience, and the experience of many others, that they do much to *guarantee* the fulfillment of your own special requests.

When you read them, you will see that they are all positive in nature and contain nothing that you would not wish to have for yourself.

I have come to call them the "head of the list" goals. This is because they are already in a form you can copy . . . they start you on the task of *writing* goals instead of just "thinking about them," and they are basics which underlie all that you will add after them.

So, start your list of goals with the following:

1. Each and every day that I follow these procedures set out for my improvement, I become more *effective*, better able to *function without limitation*.
2. I pursue my goals free of any feelings of ill-will or animosity toward others. I am a warm, friendly, well-liked person. My success is *assured* and does not require me to take advantage of any other person. Rather, it *obliges* me to help others, without telling anyone about my "good deeds."
3. I see myself with the success-eye of NOW. I have discarded the failure-eye of my infancy. I am free at last of failure or limitations.

Now, add your own goals. Add *every* goal you require to bring you the needs, wants and necessary personality factors from your early lists.

Put them in your own words being careful only that they be stated as *positive, already accomplished*, and set forth in *great detail*.

Note: Because so many people find it easy to list the tangible things which they want, but hard to list the personality factors which their goals might require, I have taken the liberty of listing a few of the qualities most often necessary. Copy them on your list as they are written, or use them to help prepare your own. Most of them are goals we all need to emphasize. I learned them years ago and have made great use of them over the years. I cannot even remember how they evolved, but I can tell you they are all most helpful and effective.

Concentration. I can bring great concentration to bear upon any subject, at any time. Or, I am easily able to concentrate on any task, and am completely free of outside distraction. Or, I always work on things that count. When I have an enterprise on hand, I concentrate upon it wholly. In my concentration, the rest of the world cannot disturb me.

Efficiency. I am always efficient in everything that I undertake to do. Or, I use each minute before it has disappeared forever. I keep productive work available for odd moments. I always achieve the desired result, with a minimum of time and energy.

Courage. I face all my problems with great courage, and thus solve them much more easily.

Self-assurance. I have completely relaxed self-assurance. I am sure of myself in all situations, and with all people.

Self-respect. I respect myself and my goals and have complete self-assurance in all that I think and do. I am the equal of the best of men, and truly am capable of great accomplishments.

Perseverance. I am easily able to persevere and finish any task I undertake.

Success. I am very successful in all that I do. Because of this, I enjoy an abundance of all things, qualities, and conditions necessary to the happiness of myself and those around me. Success comes easily to me.

Honesty. I am honest with myself and therefore with everyone else.

Organization. I am well organized in every phase of my life.

Creativity. I treat all problems as opportunities to be creative and as a result my life is vastly enriched. I use creativity in every endeavor and thus enjoy a position of growing leadership. Or, I start every job by thinking how to do it better than it has been done before. Thinking in terms of a better way, I always find a better way. Or, I have an unusual ability to reach creative solutions to my problems. Knowing that I have this ability, my creative powers actively support my belief and I have a constant flow of new and good ideas.

Energy. I possess an abundant supply of energy and draw upon it at will. I know that the more energy I apply to any task, the more I have to apply to the next task. Or, I start with enthusiasm and my enthusiasm activates my energy. I work with inspiration and develop my sources of energy by continuous exercise. I find that my enthusiasm builds my energy, and my energy builds my enthusiasm. Or, I possess boundless energy and I use it freely. I realize I must give some form of energy in return for everything I receive, and gladly give it, knowing that the more energy I give, the more I have to give.

Self-improvement. I eagerly seek to improve in every phase of my life.

Memory. I have an excellent memory, not only for the immediate tasks but for all experiences that I have had. It grows better every day.

Speech. I am an excellent speaker, well prepared, logical, and completely at ease before any group. Or, I am an excellent speaker because I have knowledge of my subject and an intense desire for other people to hear it.

Reading. I read quickly and easily with great comprehension of all subject matter.

Emotions. I contact, feel, and easily show my emotions to myself and to all other people. If I'm angry, I show it and thus release it. If I'm happy, I show this. If I'm sad, I find it easy to weep and thus dispel the sadness. The ability to show emotions at appropriate times is valuable, and the mark of a mature person.

Relaxation. I am easily able to relax as deeply as I wish at any time. I use this ability to conserve my energy.

Decisiveness. I am quickly decisive in all matters, only making sure that I have complete and accurate data before acting. Or, I make decisions quickly. I know that by deciding quickly, I make the best decisions. I always know what to do next. By deciding everything quickly, I am tremendously productive. Or, my decisive qualities are always awake to challenge. The more difficult the problem, the more eagerly I respond to the task, and the more my intelligence is stimulated.

Self-liking. I like myself very much indeed at all times. Since this thought precedes my actions, I am consistently pleased with my behavior.

Goals. My goals are high, and I reach them easily and quickly by affirming them constantly. I am dynamic in my self-improvement because I am consistent in my efforts.

Maturity. I am a mature person and consequently seek ever greater growth within myself. I know that everyone around me is benefited by the evidence of my maturity.

Foresight. I work with foresight. I have this foresight because my plans are built on ideals which maintain my enthusiasm to get things done.

Composure. I have complete composure at all times. I accept challenge and arguments calmly and in good spirit. I recognize that disagreement is an inevitable outgrowth when groups of people engage in the problem-solving process.

Interest in people. I meet people easily and enjoy each new association. My deep sincerity puts people at ease and stimulates their confidence. Or, I am sincerely interested in people. I find each new personality has some unique quality which enriches my experience.

Loyalty. I am loyal to all who depend on me.

Planning. I always plan my work. I organize my efforts today, for tomorrow, and the future. I work with my goals in mind. I plan ahead to get ahead.

Accomplishment. I take pride in a job well done. Accomplishment is my greatest reward. I always do more than I get paid for, so that I ultimately get paid for more than I do.

Work for quality. I work for quality. I have the patience to do simple things perfectly and thereby strengthen my skill to do difficult things easily.

Self-starting. I always do things as they need to be done. I start vigorously and promptly each day on each new task. My energetic starts make me an achiever.

Self-education. I know that leaders are readers. I systematically study books and magazines which increase my earning power.

Motivation of others. I successfully train others to do my work. I give those who help me generous credit for their accomplishments. The willing support of other people is essential to my success.

Self-discipline. I know that I can do what I have to do, and I have to do what I have set out to do.

Goal direction. Every day my goals are nearer because I stay on the main highway. I practice resolute self-denial and keep my attention on my goals until I achieve them.

Industry. I am habitually industrious and get things done. My attitude is always "will do" as well as "can do."

Calm and cheerful. I am calm and cheerful. I share my inner peace and happiness with others.

In order to assist you in this very important task of selecting personality factors to be your goals, let me assist you further by asking you a few simple questions and then show you what personality factors your answers indicate you need. Answer yes or no *without* looking at the analysis.

	Yes	No
1. Should people have to pay school taxes if they do not have children?	☐	☐
2. I try to see what others think before I take a stand.	☐	☐
3. I would rather have people dislike me than look down on me.	☐	☐
4. I must admit I am a pretty fair talker.	☐	☐

Analysis: **LEADERSHIP** is the quality indicated, and to the extent your answers match those given, you *have* the quality. To the extent they *do not* match, you should make it your goal.

1—yes, 2—no, 3—yes, 4—yes.

	Yes	No
5. Do you read at least 10 books a year?	☐	☐
6. When faced with a problem, do you find you act on impulse to solve it?	☐	☐
7. Do you like science?	☐	☐
8. Do you feel teachers often expect too much from their students?	☐	☐

Analysis: **INTELLECTUAL EFFICIENCY** is at stake here. To the extent your answers match those given, you have and use it. To the extent your answers do not match, you might consider it as a goal.

5—yes, 6—no, 7—yes, 8—no.

9. Do you always try to do a little better than what is expected of you? ☐ ☐
10. Did you like it very much when one of your papers was read to the class in school? ☐ ☐
11. Do you believe that in many ways the poor man is better off than the rich man? ☐ ☐
12. Do you believe that planning your activities in advance is likely to take most of the fun out of them? ☐ ☐

Analysis: **AMBITION** is reflected in your answers. You should put it on your list if your answers vary too much from those given.

9—yes, 10—yes, 11—no, 12—no.

13. Do you feel that when prices are high that you can't blame someone for getting all he can while the getting is good? ☐ ☐
14. Do you feel every family owes it to the city to keep its sidewalks cleared of snow in the winter and its lawn mowed in the summer? ☐ ☐
15. Do you feel we ought to take care of ourselves and let everybody else take care of themselves? ☐ ☐
16. Do you feel any guilt or shame if you fail to vote in the elections? ☐ ☐

Analysis: **RESPONSIBILITY** is the character or personality factor indicated by your answers. To the extent your answers fail to match, you need to add it to your goals.

13—no, 14—yes, 15—no, 16—yes.

17. Do you think there are as many opportunities for an ambitious person as there ever were? ☐ ☐
18. Do you often have doubts as to what action will win approval for you in your work? ☐ ☐
19. Do you doubt that you will ever be an important person? ... that you will make a real contribution to the world? ☐ ☐
20. Do you get nervous and upset when you feel you have been placed in competition with another? ☐ ☐

Analysis: **CONVICTION OF SUCCESS** is tested here, and failure to match the answers indicates a need to add an affirmation of success to every one of your goals.

17—yes, 18—no, 19—no, 20—no.

I hope these examples of self-examination have helped you ferret out a few of your hidden needs. Now, check your goals again . . . and *put them on paper.*

As you do, and as you move ahead to the next step, I must give you one word of caution.

WARNING!

Don't tell anyone *about* your program, your new goals, your hopes for the future except someone taking the steps with you! This is of the utmost importance as you begin. Your frame of mind at this critical point can easily be infected with doubt, just as a tiny, new-born infant could fall prey to disease.

Give yourself a chance by giving no one the opportunity to keep you from the wealth and success which can be yours.

When you have started to achieve that success . . . they will be asking for your secret. Now, they have to deny it or admit their own lack of qualifications. Take no chances!

The Next Step — DAILY DECLARATIONS

As set forth earlier in these pages, the form of your goals has been determined as positive, already accomplished, complete.

They have been written in the proper form and include everything in the world you really want together with every personal quality you might need to acquire and enjoy them.

Now the process of actually acquiring all these things begins. It begins with DAILY DECLARATIONS. Here is how they are undertaken:

EACH MORNING:

1. Immediately upon awakening, read your list of goals as prepared in their positive, accomplished form.
   Read every one of them. Read aloud if at all possible. If this cannot be done, then move your lips and form the words silently as you read. (This adds another physical dimension to the intellectual declaration.)

2. After you have read each declaration . . . pause . . . *visualize it completely.* In your mind's eye, SEE the car, the home, the office with your name on the door. Touch the steering wheel, walk through the door. Feel the money from that first paycheck in your hands *in cash*, count it, see each bill and know its denomination.

EACH EVENING:

Just before you retire . . . *no matter how late it is, no matter how tired you are,* repeat the morning process.

Because it is *essential* that the Daily Declarations be carried out completely and in the most effective manner, let me give you an example of just two properly worded goals and the proper way of declaring them. As you will see, one is a declaration concerning a physical property, the other a personality quality.

We start with the need for $850 to pay an overdue debt and the desire *(want)* for greater confidence.

Correctly stated those listed "wishes" became the following *goals:*

1. The $850 bill from Smith & Company is paid in full.
2. I face each day supremely confident of my ability to handle every detail of my thoughts and activities. I am certain of my capacity to perform in a superior manner.

When making the Daily Declarations, the first one will be read aloud. Then the declarant will *visualize* the bill in question with "Paid in Full" stamped across it. Or, if the bill itself is in the possession of the declarant, it is taken in hand . . . examined . . . the declaration is stated again and the bill is turned face down. Again the declaration is stated aloud.

In the personality quality declaration: it is first read aloud, giving thought to the exact meaning of each word. Then the declarant *visualizes* a situation in which that quality—self-confidence perhaps—would be important. (Attempting a sale, trying to convince a superior, etc.). Now, *visualize* the situation as the declarant would *like* it to occur. The declarant shows great self-confidence; this confidence is sufficient to bring about the desired result. The visualization has produced a *correct* image in the subconscious. Then, when you are faced with the *real* situation, you will have this positive material to draw on rather than the "failures" that were the only information available before.

This process is to be carried on for *every single goal on your lists.*

This process of Daily Declarations is *absolutely essential* to your successful practice of Dyna/Psyc.

It is not necessary that you understand completely WHY it works. It is only important that you practice it long enough to learn (as thousands of others have learned) that it does work! For now, merely accept that fact as you accept the antibiotic from your doctor without a detailed understanding of the scientific reasons for its effectiveness.

A Note To Skeptics: Generally, at this point, in the examination of Dyna/Psyc, a handful of would-be practitioners begin to grumble things like: "mumbo-jumbo," "day-dreams," "sounds ridiculous" or words to that effect.

If you are in that number, let me suggest this—*suspend your skepticism and give yourself a chance.* Notice I said "give *yourself* a chance." I am not concerned for Dyna/Psyc. Your doubts cannot harm it one iota. It works; the wealth that I and others have achieved using the method has proven time and time again that *it works!* But your skeptical refusal to at least TRY will once again *deprive you* of the success you want so badly but which continues to elude you.

Look at it this way. At the most, you have nothing to *lose* but a little time. You have a world of wealth and happiness to *gain.* Surely, with the odds so overwhelming—i.e. nothing vs. EVERYTHING — it's worth trying.

To be unwilling to *try* is to cut yourself off from at least the possibility of success for the dubious pleasure of *never knowing* what might have happened.

CHAPTER SIX

HOW LONG WILL IT TAKE?

The answer to that question lies in assessing the following factors:

How long did it take you to build your Inadequate Self Image?

How bad a self image do you have?

Are you secretly afraid of success?

How burdened are you with guilt from past failures?

Are you consistently making your Daily Declarations?

Are you really *seeing* when you attempt to visualize?

Are you suspending skepticism?

Are you prepared to leave yesterday behind and live TODAY with your Daily Declarations?

How much time and effort are you willing to give your progress?*

*On the next page we will give you the answer to "Can you Speed up the Progress?"

Can You Speed Up the Progress?

Yes! Yes, there is a method to bring about the wanted changes in your life at an even faster rate than you can achieve through your Daily Declarations alone.

While it is similar in nature to the use of Daily Declarations, it is somewhat different in use and application and totally different in the *degree of power* generated.

You might think of the comparison between the two by thinking of the Daily Declarations as the ordinary 110-volt current which is used to power electric lights and small appliances in your home. The power of *Super Suggestion,* which we are going to discuss, is then like the 220-volt current which is used to power heavy machinery or bigger home appliances which require far more energy.

Super Suggestion carries a far greater charge of power. For that reason it is capable of moving your progress forward at a *far faster* rate than the Daily Declarations alone. Used *together,* the two kinds of motivating power, Daily Declarations and Super Suggestion, assure the most rapid results possible.

Before outlining the use of Super Suggestion and showing how it works, it is well to consider its limitations.

Super Suggestion can *only* be used on the *intangible* goals you are seeking. You can use it to build yourself, bring about in yourself the personality factors which make for success. But, you *must not use it* for the acquisition of *things.* The realities which Super Suggestion creates in your subconscious mind must be limited to *intangibles* or you can do great harm to your ability to reach chosen goals.

Here's why: Super Suggestion creates full-belief even before the subject goal has been achieved. This is fine with the mental, emotional, and behavioral patterns you are seeking. Once you behave as though *these intangible changes have already occurred,* they dictate your behavior and you reap the benefits.

But, if the subconscious is assured (through Super Suggestion) that you *already have* the salary, the house, the car you are seeking, your entire subconscious mental levels *cease to help you acquire them.*

Remember, we said that the subconscious works without logic; it is an uncritical force. When we declare in our fully conscious state that we have things we are seeking, our conscious mind *knows* of their future state and "edits" the information it passes on to the lower levels of our consciousness. Then all systems will work to help us acquire them.

The difference can be summed up in this manner:

DAILY DECLARATIONS

To be used *at* least twice a day (when you awaken and before you go to sleep) and as many additional times as you wish. Put the most important ones on a card you can carry with you and read aloud (or at least move your lips) and *visualize* as often as you can.

Used for *both:* (1) Personality and character growth toward your *intangible* goals (courage, efficiency, creativity, organization, etc.); (2) The attainment of the material, *tangible* things you need for your happiness and comfort (money, house, car, boat, etc.).

SUPER SUGGESTION

To be used only *once* a day, *every* day. Pick a time that's usually convenient: before lunch for example.

Used *only* for the *intangible* goals. *Not* for "things."

BECAUSE:

This powerful force "plugs in" directly to the lower levels of our consciousness.

Trying to use *Super Suggestion* for "things" would be like plugging your record player into the high voltage outlet meant for your electric stove. The record player wouldn't function.

How To Deep Condition and Use SUPER SUGGESTION

In order to understand the necessary steps you must take so that you can use Super Suggestion, it is necessary that we examine *how* and *why* it works. To help you do this I have made the graph on the following page. It attempts to demonstrate the *levels of consciousness* which all of us may experience at one time or another.

As you can see, at one end of the scale is 100% consciousness—a wide-awake, alert condition in which there would also be some degree of muscular tension.

One of the best examples of this condition of *full* consciousness might be at the moment of participation at top level of efficiency in some sport involving careful attention, speedy reactions, muscular energy, etc.

At the very opposite end of the scale is a deep coma. An unconsciousness so complete that the person cannot even be aroused from it medically.

As you examine the various degrees of consciousness, imagine if you will how you would react at each stage to *suggestions* from a source outside your own body.

The top-form sports champion, intent and alert is not swayed from what he is doing even by shouts from spectators. His own mind is in full control of his consciousness. He is not about to take *suggestions* from unskilled members of the watching crowd.

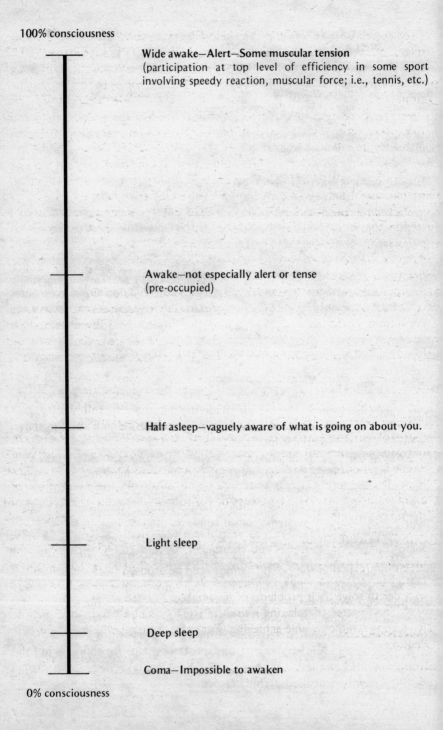

100% consciousness

Wide awake—Alert—Some muscular tension
(participation at top level of efficiency in some sport involving speedy reaction, muscular force; i.e., tennis, etc.)

Awake—not especially alert or tense
(pre-occupied)

Half asleep—vaguely aware of what is going on about you.

Light sleep

Deep sleep

Coma—Impossible to awaken

0% consciousness

Yet, the same athlete, awakened from a sound sleep, still drowsy, might be fooled into running for an exit with the false suggestion, "GET OUT OF HERE, THE ROOM'S ON FIRE!" And every muscle of his body would then be reacting, *not to his own conscious mind*, but to the suggestion!

These two examples: *suggestion rejection* on the playing field and *suggestion acceptance* in the half-awake state, can be very helpful to our effective use of Super Suggestion.

Note that in both cases the *same mind* was the subject of an outside suggestion. The only differences were the *condition of consciousness* at the moment of suggestion *and* the *power* of the suggestion.

In the suggestion *rejection* case we had a *fully conscious*, concentrated mind. The suggestion was but one of many shouts, with little chance of penetrating the subject's consciousness.

In the *accepted* suggestion situation, the level of consciousness was far down our scale. Thus, it was more readily accessible to the suggestion. And the suggestion itself was clear, urgent and without outside interference.

Preparing to use Super Suggestion, we set up the suggestion-acceptance conditions which are best for reaching the "open" level of consciousness and presenting the suggestion in the most "powerful" manner.

Therefore, when you are first learning to use Super Suggestion it is best to:

1. Condition yourself in a *quiet, darkened* room.
2. Sit in a comfortable position and relax your muscles.
3. Close your eyes.

Taking these steps you reduce many of the consciousness factors of our athletic friend in the suggestion-rejection example, i.e.: folding your hands in your lap or resting them on the chairarms causes you to reduce muscular tension. Closing your eyes, you close off the perception of extraneous matters. The quietness of the room reduces the distractions of the noise around you.

Note! Do not lie down as you prepare or condition yourself to use Super Suggestion. Since, as you could check on our graph, you are moving to a lowered level of consciousness it would be very easy to fall asleep. In fact, I have known many people who use a Super Suggestion of sleeping in order to solve their problems of insomnia.

This matter of relaxing *muscular* tension is one which some people have considerable trouble achieving. For them, I suggest the following procedure:

As you are sitting in your chair, visualize the various parts of your body. Start with the very tips of your toes. *Think* of them relaxing . . . slowly, gradually, relaxing. Proceed up your body, a section at a time, thinking of the specific part and *feeling* it relax. Don't *make* it relax. *Let* it relax. By the time you have reached the top of your head, you will be in good *muscular* relaxation.

Muscular relaxation completed, you are already half-way through the *mental conditioning* which is the balance of the conditioning preparation required for Super Suggestion. Because the very *suggestion process* used to relax those muscles has also been establishing mental relaxation as well.

Now, begin to count, silently, slowly, feeling yourself slip gently downward to a perfect conditioning level of consciousness. You will count from 1 down to 20. At 20, you *will* be where you need to be.

Once this physical-mental conditioning is completed, you begin to use the Super Suggestion material you already prepared for this session before going into your room and commencing the conditioning.

Preparing your Super Suggestion

Unlike your Daily Declarations in which you work on everything on your list of goals, Super Suggestion is used on just *one intangible* quality at a time.

First, select one of the basic personality or character qualities from your intangible goals. Since you must work with only one at a time, making your choice should be based on the most important quality first. You will continue to use only that one quality for Super Suggestion until you have attained it. But, I promise you it will be attained in far less time than you can imagine. Super Suggestion works wonders!

Of course, you have reworded your wish for the quality into a present and positive form as a goal. Now, select from the wording of the goal two or three *key words* to act as sort of "code" for the entire goal. You do this so that you do not have to commit the entire declaration to memory. (Remember, you will use Super Suggestion with your eyes closed.)

You will read the entire declaration each time *before* you begin the process of "conditioning" down into a lower level of consciousness. Once there you will repeat the "key" or "code" words and that will be all that is necessary. The speaking of those words, while in the requisite "conditioned" state, will *implant the entire declaration* with a force and power beyond your prior imaginings!

Putting it All Together

Let me now list for clarity the entire procedure for using Super Suggestion:

1. You have prepared a *single* intangible (character, behavior, or personality) goal. The one quality you feel you need most.

2. You have selected a Key word or two to use as a "code" in your lower level suggestion effort.

3. Now you go into a dimly-lit or darkened room, close the door, seat yourself comfortably to relax every muscle.

4. Read the full declaration slowly and carefully. Remember the "key words" from it as you begin to condition yourself into a lower level of consciousness.

5. Go into your lower level of consciousness as outlined previously.

6. Repeat the key words *silently*, to yourself to implant the declaration at the lower level.

7. Return to your fully conscious level, thinking as you do that you are going to feel more alert, more relaxed, more energetic than you ever have before.

That's it! That's all there is to do, and you are putting Super Suggestion to work! The desired effect will come before you know it. How soon? That depends on how well you learn to "count yourself down" into deep relaxation . . . and the frequency and consistency with which you perform both your Daily Declarations and utilize Super Suggestion.

The only way to know you are effectively using your Daily Declarations is to follow the instructions to *declare them every day . . . at least twice a day*. But, how can you know you are reaching the proper depth of consciousness for effective use of Super Suggestion?

This is difficult to define exactly. For it is a highly personal or subjective "feeling" which, when achieved, is evidence of the proper state. However, it is not a condition similar to the lit or un-lit light bulb. It is *not* a completely "on" or "off" state.

Therefore, as you approach the essential level, you are "fading in" on it. The deeper you descend, the closer you are to the ultimate level. But Super Suggestion used anyplace along the spectrum will be effective. It will be effective in direct ratio to the degree of conditioning you have reached.

Simply put, you need not worry about your Suggestions "not working" because you have not yet developed the ability to go quickly and surely to the deeper level of consciousness. They will work better as you increase your efficiency in this conditioning, but they will be "working" for you all the time you are improving.

For *practice* is the secret of more efficient or more effective conditioning for Super Suggestion. Some people will find it easier than others (just as some people take to swimming or golf rapidly and with greater ease than others). But YOU will develop an ever-increasing facility for rapid and effective descent to the lower level of consciousness as you repeat the experience.

How does it feel? There are as many answers to this question as there are people who have tried it. However, their answers all contain certain elements: relaxed, almost no body-feeling, a little drowsy perhaps, sounds fade away. You will be aware that you are you; you will not be unconscious, but you will be remote from the press of normal everyday sensation and thought.

And it is important for you to know that you will be able to reach this relaxed condition with greater and greater speed and less and less effort as you practice it. Like the ability we develop to run rapidly along a well-known path where at first we could only inch our way.

One word of caution! Don't try too hard. This defeats the very effort itself. This is a *relaxing* effort . . . NOT a *concentrating* effort. *Let* yourself go . . . don't try to *make* yourself descend!

At this point I want to remind you that this conditioning to a lower level of consciousness and using Super Suggestion is ONLY for the intangible goals, for changing qualities of basic character, personality, behavior. You don't use this method to acquire the new car, the larger salary, the new home. These goals all *require* a certain amount of time. But *personality changes* can be made as rapidly as you can Super Suggest them.

In addition to the basic and lasting personality changes which we can effect through repeated Super Suggestion, you will be able to use this method of conditioning to achieve many short-term advantages.

Temporary uses to which this capacity has been put include:

Fear of the Dentist.	—Used before the visit, fear gone!
Late night, important work to complete, too tired.	—Super Suggestion of alertness and concentration provides both.
Long drive, sleepy.	—Two or three minutes of a Super Suggestion of alertness at side of the road. Perfectly able to continue.
Interview for new job, fright and feeling of panic.	—Brief descent and Super Suggestion of calm and poise. Problem gone for interview.
Can't sleep at night.	—In bed, a Super Suggestion of sleep, deep and restful. Success!

| Pain (Dentist, childbirth, etc.) | —Used by one proficient in the pre-paratory conditioning . . . no pain. |

Coming Out

A *plus factor* which you can add to your conditioning when you begin to develop some degree of ease in its practice is *enhancement of later consciousness.*

This is a simple process by means of which you will return to the high consciousness level feeling *refreshed,* with new energy, vigor. Your mental outlook will be happier and more confident than it was *before* you conditioned for Super Suggestion.

Adding this factor is simply a matter of *counting backwards* as you begin your return from the point of suggestion — 20 . . . 19 . . . 18 . . . etc. As you pass 10 and again at 5, tell yourself silently of the conditions that will be yours when you reach zero.

In other words, as you are arising from the lower level of conscious-ness, you make double use of the trip. Not only do you strongly implant the Super Suggestion, but on the way up, you emphasize the *energetic feeling of power and well being* which *will be yours* once you return to full consciousness.

A final point—when and how often do you use Super Suggestion in preparing to achieve a basic "personal quality" goal? As an aid to reaching the fullest efficiency of self-conditioning at the lower level, you need not limit the number of times you practice it daily. But, as a matter of *effect-ively* using a single Super Suggestion, you'll get the maximum benefit from a once-a-day use. However, you can—and should—use the Super Suggestion technique for emergencies (a trip to the dentist, a job interview, etc.).

The best time to use this powerful aid to achieving your intangible goals is when you are not tired and are reasonably alert. Thus, it becomes clear that the first thing in the morning, late at night, or just after eating *are not* the times to condition. If possible, perhaps just before your lunch-eon period, or just after work if you are on a tight working schedule. Otherwise, any period you can set aside while you're wide-awake.

Summary

This now gives you two of the important tools which make Dyna/Psyc effective:

DAILY DECLARATIONS and SUPER SUGGESTION.

As you can see, they work in the *conscious* and *subconscious* levels of our mind.

In the next chapter we examine the *third* and *most powerful* tool Dyna/Psyc has to offer you.

CHAPTER SEVEN

YOUR UNCONSCIOUS COMPUTER

Decision-making is the most significant work you ever do. That is because it is impossible for the human animal to even *exist* without a steady stream of decisions.

The decision to eat or drink and the choice of what you will eat or drink is a simplified example of the decision-making process to which we give little or no importance but which is essential to our continued existence.

Other than breathing, the beating of the heart, etc., the bodily functions are generally carried on after making a decision or a series of decisions. Think of the number of decisions, each tiny and insignificant, but each essential in the process of merely scratching your nose.

First, there's the awareness of the itch. Then, the decision: to rub with the back of your hand? Or rub with your sleeve? Scratch with your fingers? Which fingers of which hand? Now hard, how long? Is the selected hand free to scratch or must some burden in the hand be set down or shifted to the other hand before scratching? These are merely the highlights of the number of decisions that can enter into a simple act.

And that is only part of it. In addition to making the *basic decision* to scratch, we must make *innumerable calculations* in order to effectively carry out the decisions; i.e., how far to lift the hand, the planned trajectory which will bring the fingers, flexing and unflexing properly into just the exact position on the nose we cannot see. From a calculation standpoint, we are something like plotting a rendezvous in space between two spacecraft.

The hardware which the space agency has developed for such command and guidance is complex almost beyond belief. And yet, a single day's activity of an average, active human body requires that decisions and computations be made which are *so numerous* and must be made with *so much complex input* of information and in such *short periods of time that no computer in existence could handle it.*

Plotting and executing a space voyage is not one bit as complex as your decision and computing problems in driving downtown through busy traffic as you go to work each day. You make *more decisions* based on *more information inputs* and must make more instantaneous calculations of speed, proximity, even potential personality of other drivers ("—that s.o.b. won't let me in here") in a half-hour drive than any flight to the moon.

In short, the message is brief. NO MAN-MADE CALCULATOR OR COMPUTER EVEN BEGINS TO APPROACH THE COMPLEXITY OR EFFICIENCY OF THE HUMAN MIND.

The final step in the implementation of Dyna/Psyc—and the changing of your life—is the creation of CONSCIOUS ACCESS TO THE COMPUTER OF YOUR UNCONSCIOUS MIND!

Make no mistake, *ordinary people* never learn to use the great Unconscious Computer. The day they learn to use it, they cease to be *ordinary*.

Searching the writings of famous men, the statements they have made as to their *source of creativity* (which is essentially a matter of decision-making) and reading everything I could find in this area, I can tell you this:

Edison, Einstein, Mozart, Emerson, Tchaikovsky, Steinmetz, James Watt and innumerable other inventors, scientists, writers, composers all have given evidence of their *using the great Unconscious Computer* that exists in all of us. They each somehow *happened upon* this great resource. YOU are going to learn how to use it *knowingly* and *at will*.

What Will It Do For You?

I   *Provide meaningful and productive answers to your problems.*
II   *Increase the efficiency and well-being of your mind itself.*
III   *Furnish the POWER that turns your Daily Declarations into actual possessions.*

I   In the PROBLEM area, we all know that the burden of decision-making (which is what problems are . . . difficult decisions) increases in direct ratio to their complexity. If the decision is yes or no, stay or go, black or white, it is usually less complex than if there are *several* possible solutions and you must decide which is the best course of action.

Immediately we are faced with a *lot* of information of varying degrees of importance, a *number* of answers of varying worth and, very often, emotional pressures to make one decision or another. In short, a "computer-like" problem.

Using our unconscious power we can *have the answer computed and delivered to us!*

II   MENTAL WELL-BEING comes into focus when we understand how the Unconscious Computer can be used to reduce stress and tension in the nervous system. Permit me to quote from a work I read some years ago:

> "Recent research on sleep has reversed some of the fashionable conceptions which were widely discussed in years past. The fact is that, although the number of hours required varies slightly between individuals and also varies with age, the idea that only four or five hours are actually required is fallacious. New findings point up that your actual requirement conforms more closely to your common practice of sleeping seven, eight, or nine hours than was previously thought. Assuming that your true requirement is eight hours, then the first half, or approximately four hours, is devoted to your body repairs or the rejuvenation of the tissues which have been worn down during the day. Scientists, in making observations of this period, note that during the first hour, sleep is particularly deep and there is an accompanying increase in basal metabolism. There is an extra expenditure of energy involved in the first hurried elimination of the major aspects of purely physical fatigue. The second, third, and fourth hours produce somewhat lighter sleep and require considerably less energy, while the more intricate physical repairs are accomplished—such things as reflexes and various physically-derived judgments such as distance, form, and color are thus returned to normal through cell repair and reproduction."

Since this is the case, it is *imperative* that you have some method of *reducing the tension and pressures* which modern day living places upon us.

The use of the Unconscious Computer *can be put to work* to clear your mental system of each day's problems *as you sleep* and *prepare your mind* for the following day's activities.

III   DECLARATION ACHIEVEMENT is accomplished through the use of this same Unconscious Computer.

Here is how that works. As your Daily Declarations are made, the unconscious computer receives that information from you. It becomes the function of this giant calculator to *devise the methods* that you can use to get those goals!

I will show you how to be able to *receive* those solutions or answers as they have been calculated.

Every time you had a "hunch" that solved a problem for you, you were using this power. When a name was "on the tip of your tongue" but you couldn't think of it, haven't you often told someone . . . "I'll think of it on the way home." And then, just as you said you would, you "remembered" it later? That too was an example of the use of this power.

Those people who, when faced with an important decision, decide to "sleep on it" and awaken the next day with the answer are *unconsciously* using their computer.

But I want *you* to be able to use it *consciously,* not by accident.

The hardest job I'll have in getting you to put this fabulous power to work is getting you to *try.* That's because the method of using it is so simple, seems so easy, many persons are totally unable to accept it. I hope *you* don't suffer from that limitation.

Putting the Unconscious Computer to Work

The three key words for putting your U/C to work are:

WRITE — TRY — ASK

WRITE: Write out your problem. This may sound foolish, but my experience has shown that a great number of problems exist *only* because they have not been clearly defined or outlined.

Once you actually write out the problem, you are going to find that you will see it in a new light. On your paper start with the words, "Shall I do this . . .?"

Carefully, fully, yet concisely, state the problem to which you are seeking an answer.

TRY: Try to answer it yourself. On the piece of paper which contains your stated problem, place two columns. In one column put all the reasons *for* taking the particular step. In the other, all the reasons *against.*

Put in enough time doing this that you are relatively certain that you cannot solve the problem *consciously.*

Once you are forced to reach the decision that you *cannot* solve the problem consciously, go to step three.

ASK: Ask your Unconscious Computer to solve it for you. This is the part of the procedure which many people find hard to accept.

They simply cannot believe that any task of such magnitude could be carried on by simply "asking" part of your mind to take care of it.

And yet, these same people drive a car to work every morning, many times becoming so involved in their own *conscious* thoughts that they are letting their Unconscious Computer *do all the driving*.

They will suddenly become aware, almost like someone awakening from sleep, that they are ready to turn off the freeway or Turnpike. They will be unable to recall clearly the specifics of what occurred in connection with their wending their way through traffic.

ACCEPT IT! Think of your U/C as another person, an employee or assistant. Just say to that force . . . "I want the answer to this problem by tomorrow morning . . . or four o'clock this afternoon." Or, if it is particularly difficult, give the computer more time. Tell it you want the answer by next Saturday or something of the sort.

Then, FORGET IT! Forget the problem completely. Your computer *will not* work on a problem while *you* are working on it in your conscious mind. It is as though you had to release all the figures on some job to another person before he could go to work on it.

So, *forget it* once you have asked the Unconscious Computer to solve it for you. And you *can* forget it because your Unconscious Computer *will* solve it!

Simple as the use of this powerful force is, there are a number of questions which people have asked me concerning it. I have set them forth below, together with my answers, in case you too are wondering the same things.

Q. Doesn't someone have to have a really *brilliant* mind for this to work?

A. No. It can work for anyone if he will merely follow the three steps outlined.

Q. Are there any limitations on using the Unconscious Computer?

A. Only those I set forth already. First, that the problem must be written out in a clear, complete form. Second, *you* must go through the steps of *trying consciously* to solve it. *You must put on paper* the various "pro's" and "con's" which you can find.

Q. How do you decide "when" the computer must give you the answer?

A. Don't "put-off" a decision which really needs to be made. But don't try to "kid" the computer. If you don't have to make the decision for some time, don't give the computer a false deadline. "Need" seems to be an important element in the speedy functioning of this power. Also, the "when" is seldom a problem IF you have honestly gone through steps one and two. The dimensions of the problem and the quantity of material for and against the decision will influence your timetable as well as your *need* for the answer at a particular time.

Q. How and Why does it work?

A. There are a number of theories put forth by psychologists, psychiatrists, even mystics and religious teachers. I don't really know. I simply know that it *does work*.

The success this method has given me is the recommendation I offer for your trying it. It does work! That's all I ever really needed to know about it.

Q. Why is it important?

A. Because really effective people cannot afford to go around carrying dozens of unsolved problems in their minds. They need the free use of their consciousness to take care of the matters of the moment. Yet, they also encounter larger problems that they are *unable* to readily solve for themselves *even after* defining them, laying them out fully, and going over the pros and cons.

Unsolved problems are worries! Worries are destructive.

Q. What is its greatest value?

A. The fact that you are able to use the greatest part of your mind, a secret part, unaccessible to most people . . . *at will!* There is no question that the unconscious part of our mind (for reasons I still do not completely understand) has a capacity for creativity, problem-solving, etc. *far beyond* the other portions of the mental equipment. The Unconscious Computer is truly a *super power*. Its relationship to our conscious mind is like comparing a single man's efforts with those of a computer.

Q. Can it only be used on a basis where the answer will not be forthcoming for some time?

A. No. There is a technique for nearly "instant" application. All you have to do is "condition" yourself as though you were preparing to use Super Suggestion. At that level, ask the U/C your question. If, prior to this step you have defined the problem and tried consciously to solve it by weighing the opposing advantages and disadvantages, you will only have to wait a bit in that deeper state of consciousness and the answer will come.

Q. How will I know the answer?

A. First, let me explain you will not begin to hear mysterious "voices." It is just that the solution to the problem will come to you in a form immediately capable of application to your problem.

It will "feel" like the *right* answer. You will also "feel" you want to get right back to the problem and put that answer to work at once.

If you have had some mental "block" that kept you from seeing the solution at an earlier stage, the "answer" may have to come to you in a "disguise." That is, something may keep coming to your mind in connection with the problem which *seems* to have no application. A snatch of an old song, a childhood game, etc. But then it will suddenly occur to you that *"Bye Bye Blackbird"* may be an unconscious suggestion to get rid of the *source* of the problem. And that will be one of the two courses you had been trying to decide between.

Generally, the feeling of "rightness" and the feeling of "eagerness" to carry out the solution are all you will need to identify the correct answer from the Unconscious Computer.

Q. Can I do this right away . . . or does it take a few tries to get it working?

A. It will respond when you properly prepare and ask. However, as you continue to use it, proficiency will grow as it does with all familiar things.

But, if it *doesn't work at all*, YOU ARE PREVENTING ITS FUNCTION! It won't work if you consciously KNOW it won't. Accept that it will! And I assure you . . . it *does!*

A Word of Warning: Don't fail to act on the answer you are given! Or you will find it is some time before it will function again!

The Second Aspect of the Unconscious Computer

As we have noted earlier there are three ways in which your U/C can be put to work to great advantage.

We have examined one—the *problem solving* capacity. Now, let us consider its use as an aid to mental health and increasing your general efficiency.

During your hours of sleep, your *unconscious* works (primarily through the use of dreams) to lower the tensions and pressures which have accumulated during the day.

However, that function is only carried on *after* the process of *physical* rehabilitation is carried out during the first four hours or so of your sleep.

If the day's problems, pressures, tensions have been particularly heavy—*or* if you just didn't get enough sleep during the night—your mental rehabilitation may be incomplete upon awakening.

This means you will face the new day with a lowered tolerance to the day's demands on your nervous/mental capacities. Irritability makes itself felt, problems loom larger than life-size.

And, when you are at your lowest ebb the next day (for we all seem to have "cycles" of more energy, less energy, etc. in regular patterns throughout our waking hours) your reserves are shot and you're in trouble.

It is at this point that you can utilize your U/C to give yourself what I call the *Silent Treatment*.

This *Silent Treatment* is a method of permitting your U/C to "catch-up" for a brief time on the chores it was unable to complete the night before.

It enables you to spend *just a few minutes* in a special manner which will increase your efficiency in every way for hours!

And what will you be doing during that few minutes? Nothing!

Here's how to give yourself this rewarding *Silent Treatment:*

1. Make a *conscious determination* that the time has come for a treatment. Don't just let yourself "happen" into it. Tell yourself you are going to turn things over to the U/C for a time.

2. Sit down, or if possible, lie down. Close your eyes and *step outside of yourself.* Lying there with your eyes closed become as though you were a passive spectator of yourself. Don't *try* to think of anything . . . don't try *not* to think of anything. Relax . . . just exist for the moment with closed eyes. Think of yourself as having "stepped aside" while some workmen carry on an important task of "cleaning-up" the area where you have been working. Just *relax* while they put everything in order for your return after a while. Just sit or lie with eyes closed and . . . let go!

3. When you feel an almost uncontrollable desire to *open your eyes* . . . do so. This will be somewhere from five to twenty minutes later.

Here are the results you can expect from Silent Treatments: You will find increased enthusiasm, energy, and an over all increase in your sense of well-being. Tiredness falls away.

These results will *increase* in effect after you have been giving yourself a daily treatment for a week or two.

But a warning. Sometimes, just as you open your eyes, it is such a pleasant experience you have just had, you might think of closing them again for a time. *Don't!* A second Silent Treatment, immediately upon the heels of the first, is sure to not only *undo* the benefits of the first, it will leave you feeling *terrible.* You will probably have a headache. One treatment only. That's the rule.

Remember, the Silent Treatment does not involve *sleep*. It is simply a means of quieting your conscious mind and permitting the unconscious to get terribly busy for a brief time. The results are well worth the trouble it may be to you to find a way to do it each day.

If you have a place at work to do it, fine. If not, perhaps you can go to your car for the few minutes required. At any rate, get comfortable; as comfortable as possible.

Another side benefit of the use of these treatments is the increasing ease with which you are able to reach your U/C. This greatly enhances the success of the problem-solving function as well.

The Third Aspect of the Unconscious Computer

This utilization of the great power of the unconscious within you requires no more effort on your part than the continued use of your *Daily Declarations.*

Just as Super Suggestion *enhances* the speed with which you can acquire a positive trait or quality which you've set up as a goal . . . the U/C also makes important contributions to goal fulfillment. Both the "things" you want and the intangible goals are conditioned into your mental apparatus.

Day by day, you will perform acts which forward you in your pursuit of those goals. Your U/C enhances the speed and certainty of your goal attainment with every decision it makes, every calculation you turn over to it. It *includes* your goal needs as one more element in making each decision.

Your U/C will *suggest* moves, ideas, strategies to you which will make your declarations realities. New and creative ideas will just seem to "come from nowhere" as you progress in the application of the natural laws of power which have been summed-up for you in Dyna/Psyc.

Be responsive to your own ideas! Forget the past when you had a tendency to immediately "put-down" an idea which came into your mind as "impractical" or "day-dreaming." Be alert and ready to be responsive to the wealth of material which your U/C can develop for you. If you turn them down, the spontaneous activity will cease. Accept them, examine them, put them into operation . . . and their supply will increase!

CHAPTER EIGHT

WHERE ARE YOU NOW?

If you have read carefully all the material presented thus far, you are 25% along the way to the Lazy Man's Wealth I promised you. Because we have set forth the basic precepts of Dyna/Psyc.

As you recall, I mentioned at the beginning that yours must be an RSVP response to this invitation to get "everything in the world you really want." R . . . you must READ it all. S . . . more than merely reading, you must STUDY it. V . . . you had to VISUALIZE the steps outlined and the steps within each step. And finally, P . . . you had to PERFORM the works as outlined.

If all you have done so far is READ, you're 25% there. To the extent you have been STUDYING what you have read, you are even further along.

Now, let us quickly review *all* the things you have to VISUALIZE and PERFORM.

I   You have DAILY DECLARATIONS. Those *positive* and *present-tense* statements made up from the lists of things (tangible and intangible) which you want and need. You are prepared to VISUALIZE them as you use them at least *twice* daily.

II   You have prepared *SUPER SUGGESTIONS* from the most important *intangible* goals. You have prepared *code words* to summon them up for use as you are in that conditioned state where you can offer suggestions to your subconscious levels.

III You are prepared to use your UNCONSCIOUS COMPUTER in three ways:
1. To solve problems
2. To give yourself SILENT TREATMENTS
3. To gain added impetus to your DAILY DECLARATIONS

Now, you are ready to establish:

IV The *daily programming* of these elements so that you receive the maximum benefit from Dyna/Psyc. To help you do this I have set up a form on which you can check off each day the necessary actions.

By all means *use it*. Do not begin your program of goal attainment without a *programmed approach* which will assist you in making all these things HABITS as soon as possible.

This is the PERFORMANCE which is the last essential to success. And, I assure you that *essential* means just that! There is simply no way to achieve the wealth you want without following through *consistently*.

Because the performing of these daily acts is so easy, requires so little time or effort, I think you must agree with me that it is indeed a "Lazy Man's Way—." Here are the Forms. They are the last thing you need to succeed.

P.S. Following them you will find a few questions many people have asked about Dyna/Psyc *after* they have begun its practice. I have included them in the hope that, as you progress, you may find among them the answers to *your* questions. They follow the forms because you do not have to read them *before* full participation in the program.

	FIRST MONTH					SECOND MONTH					THIRD MONTH				
Day	Daily Declarations		Silent Treatment	Super Suggestion	U/C Problem Solving	Daily Declarations		Silent Treatment	Super Suggestion	U/C Problem Solving	Daily Declarations		Silent Treatment	Super Suggestion	U/C Problem Solving
	A.M.	P.M.				A.M.	P.M.				A.M.	P.M.			
1															
2															
3															
4															
5															
6															
7															
8															
9															
10															
11															
12															
13															
14															
15															
16															
17															
18															
19															
20															
21															
22															
23															
24															
25															
26															
27															
28															
29															
30															
31															

Q. How many Daily Declarations do most people have?

A. The average seems to be around 20. However, the *more* you have, the better! Just be sure you use them twice daily. If the list can be handled on that basis, the number is unimportant.

Q. Why do you emphasize daily activity. Does missing a day or two hurt?

A. YES! If you are not prepared to *regularly* practice the application of the natural laws of Dyna/Psyc . . . you reduce its effect dramatically. Only consistent application pays off. But it does pay off *big!*

Q. Is one's age a handicap in practicing Dyna/Psyc?

A. Not at all. It is equally effective for teenagers or those "four-score" and older. In fact, "keeping young" has been an important goal for many.

Q. In discussing your approach with friends they said they thought I was too tense for such an effort. Isn't everybody tense?

A. More or less. Some emotion is felt by everyone at all times. The pleasant emotions make you feel good, unpleasant ones make you feel bad. Repressed emotions create tension. Dyna/Psyc makes it possible to ease the tensions of unexpressed emotions. A simple way to help reduce tension is through SILENT TREATMENTS. And suggestions of relaxation and renewed energy and enthusiasm when "coming-up" from SUPER SUGGESTION are also beneficial.

Q. What is the greatest enemy of success?

A. Fear. The fear which caused the early negative conditioning. Which, in turn, gave us an Inadequate Self Image to begin with. And fear is the worst of all tensions. It creates *anxiety* . . . which creates further tensions. Declarations for *courage, confidence, relaxation* and *effectiveness* are all helpful in controlling this threat to success.

Q. Are there any good ways to get rid of the tensions you feel at work so that you don't bring them home to "let-loose" on the family?

A. A minute or two of *any* strenuous physical activity can work like magic. Punch a bag you hang up in the garage for the purpose. Pound a few heavy nails into a piece of timber. Chop a piece of wood. Even "shadow-boxing" vigorously will relieve the tensions.

Q. Isn't it shameful for a grown man to cry?

A. Indeed not. I was once told that many psychiatrists believe the acceptance of women's tears but not of men's is one of the reasons women outlive men. Human beings should be able to *relieve* grief by this perfectly natural outlet. It has been said (and I think, truly) that those who are unable to express grief in this manner are also unable to express joy.

A childish outburst is of course inappropriate. But the inability to express emotion in some physical form is also a handicap.

Q. When a person says someone gives him a "pain in the neck" is this sometimes a literally true statement?

A. Indeed it is. There are a number of "sayings" which we hear frequently which show how deeply our emotions affect us in physical ways. "She makes me sick" . . . "I can breath easier now that the bill is paid" . . . "I've got something to get off my chest" . . . "I'm boiling mad" . . . "He gets me hot under the collar" . . . "He gives me a headache." . . . "That makes my stomach turn." These are all sayings that actually describe the physical manifestations of various emotional problems. Don't let them get to you. Use Dyna/Psyc to free yourself of the destructive tensions.

Q. How can I use Dyna/Psyc to get the support of other people?

A. You will get it *automatically* when you make your DAILY DECLARATION "I have a warm regard for others at all times and in all situations." Your success *does* require the help and cooperation of other people and a warm regard for others *communicates itself to them.* Feeling it, they *must* respond. Sometimes you will feel you have met someone who is immune to this treatment. But, persevere, you will win! And, remember this: helping others helps you rid yourself of guilt for mistakes or wrongs in your past. Guilt is a great drawback in the search for success. Rid yourself of it by unselfishly giving of yourself without fanfare or reward. It will aid you in many ways.

Q. I had barely started on my Daily Declarations when I began to feel they were not what I had really wanted. Is this wrong?

A. No. You will find your goals *change* as you progress. Merely revise your goals to conform to your new desires. Word the new ones for Daily Declaration and continue as before.

Q. Should I tell my husband the goals I have set for myself? That I'm changing my personality and character so that things will be more peaceful and happy at home?

A. No! Keep those intangible goals to yourself. As your behavior manifests the new qualities, everyone will be aware of it. But, if you talk about it, there is a too human need to call it to your attention if, as you are beginning to establish the change, you should "slip-back" to the old you for even a moment.

Remember, I have cautioned you *not* to discuss *any* of your goals or efforts with others. The main reason for this is the *energy you dissipate* by telling others of your projected changes or acquisitions. Sometimes it seems that, by telling, a person substitutes their "story" for true achievement.

Keep your own counsel! Follow the plan! Don't waste your thoughts and energies.

BOOK TWO

CHAPTER ONE

ELIMINATE THE NEGATIVE!

You can use the material in Book One to get anything you really want out of life. The only thing that's in your way is you. The old you. The old habits. The old attitudes.

The reason it's so hard to get rid of these negative forces is that they're *comfortable.* You've had them a long time. You've grown used to them. You've accepted them.

You've brainwashed yourself—or, more likely, someone has done it for you: your parents, your friends, your teachers, your boss. They meant well. They wanted you to be "happy." And their notion of happiness is that you be satisfied with things as they are.

And you accepted their definition of "happiness" because you wanted to please them.

Well, I want you to be *un*happy. Or more to the point, I want you to be *creatively unhappy.* I don't want you to accept things as they "are." I want you to make life what it *can* and *should* be.

And how will you do that? By letting Dyna/Psyc take over your life! Right now. This minute. If you say you "will" do it, you've postponed making a decision til some future date. And now is the time to act—because today is the first day of the rest of your life.

Don't waste time looking back, savoring old regrets, cherishing old mistakes, crying over lost opportunities.

When Eleanor Roosevelt was asked how she had so much energy for so many different projects, she replied, "Because I never waste time looking back."

Let's say that you had your choice of two routes to take you to work. Both were the same distance and took you the same time. But one route was along a tree-lined freeway with little traffic. And the other route was ugly, choked with traffic, bristling with stop signs—and ran right alongside a garbage dump. Which one would you take?

The first one, of course! Then why, as we go through life, do most of us take the second route—inhaling deeply as we pass yesterday's garbage, bringing the stink of yesterday's waste into today?

Because we don't know that there's another, pleasanter route to get where we're going. It *doesn't* take the same amount of time . . . it's faster! And the destination can be the one you *choose*—not the one you thought you had to accept.

Don't tell me you "can't." Because what you really mean is you "won't." And that's not you talking—it's that Inadequate Self Image . . . your ISI.

Let me show you, once again, how ISI works:

A number of years ago I handled the advertising for a Ford agency. One day, when the manager was making out the salesmen's paychecks, he commented on something that, at first, seemed unbelievable. He noted that each and every salesman earned just about the same amount each month as he had made the month before. And if there was a monthly variance, that the salesman would almost always earn, within a few percentage points, this year what he had earned the year before.

I checked into it further and found that there was an even stranger "coincidence." The Ford agency divided its sales-month into three 10-day periods. About 50% of the salesmen plugged along each day and ended up with the commission check they expected to make. Another 25% made enough sales during the *first* 10 days to provide what they anticipated as their monthly income—and never made another sale. Oh, they showed up for work all right and went through the motions, but nothing ever clicked. If you asked them what had happened, they would have told you it was "bad luck" or someone else was getting all the "buyers." The last 25% made little or no sales til the *last* 10 days of the month. Then suddenly, during those final 10 days, these salesmen got "hot."

The fact is, regardless of the pattern of sales, each salesman made what he *expected* to make. Not what he *wished* he could make or would *like* to make (and really didn't think was possible)—but what he *expected* to make. Without exception, each man got what he *really* wanted!

Let me give you another example:

Another advertising account of mine was a real estate firm. They were expanding and wanted to attract some new, top-flight salesmen. So they placed an ad that stated, truthfully, that people who were willing to come to work for them could earn $50,000 a year. The ad laid an egg. So they changed one word and had so many responses that they could pick the cream of the crop.

The word, or rather the figure, they changed was "$50,000." They made it "$20,000."

And now that you know a little bit about ISI, you can see why the first ad failed and the second ad was successful: Very few people car

70

imagine what it would be like to earn $50,000 a year. Or, more important, truly believe that they're worth that much. So they didn't even bother answering or investigating the "impossible" (for them) ad.

That's why the *prettiest* girls spend a lot of lonely nights. Most of the boys think they're "unattainable."

And here's the payoff on my true story about the real estate firm. Many of the people who couldn't imagine themselves making $50,000 a year wound up making that much and more—because the real estate firm had a training program to raise their ISI!

I mentioned that the real estate firm "picked the cream of the crop." They did—but the standards were not age, education, or experience. They picked those people who were willing to *change,* to accept the "possibility" that life could be a lot better.

Once you've picked your destination, Dyna/Psyc is the vehicle. Capable of taking you there swiftly and pleasurably. It requires only routine maintenance and that you don't cripple its performance with an ISI governor.

You don't have to understand the principle of internal combustion to drive a car. But you do have to turn on the key. I've given you the key. It's called Dyna/Psyc. Use it.

CHAPTER TWO

ACCENTUATE THE POSITIVE

I talk a lot about money. That's because it's an easy way to measure "success." As Pearl Bailey says, "I've been rich and I've been poor, but rich is better."

Not that money solves all problems. Some of the most miserable men I've known have been millionaires. They were miserable because they thought that money would make them happy. But they weren't miserable *because* they were rich. If they lost their money, they'd just be poor *and* miserable.

That's why it's important that you let Dyna/Psyc change *all* of your life, let it make you the kind of *person* you want to be and can be.

You can be a loving, forgiving, and generous person. (In fact, you can be one hell of a nice person to be around.) You can be an understanding but firm parent. You can be a true friend. You can be a trustworthy, hard-working, and loyal employee. (And if you can't, fire yourself and get another job. You'll be doing the boss and you—especially you—a big favor.) You can be a good neighbor.

You can be anything you really want to be.

And as you change, so will the people around you. Remember that if you want to teach someone to love, give them affection. If you want them to have confidence, give them encouragement. If you want them to be truthful, tell the truth. If you want them to be generous, share. If you want them to be patient, be tolerant. If you want them to be happy, give them understanding.

You can't affirm for other people. You can—and must—affirm how you *react* to them. If you allow someone to "bug" you, it's *your* problem. You may not be able to change how they act, but you *can* change how you *re*act.

However, remember Dr. Eric Berne's "The Games People Play"? You'll be surprised at how often people stop throwing the ball if you never make an effort to catch it.

Finally, accept yourself as an imperfect, fallible human being. Not that you ever stop trying to improve. But you recognize that you'll probably never quite attain 100% in all of your zones.

And when you realize—and truly *accept*—that you're imperfect, isn't it easier to accept and understand other people's imperfections?

To illustrate, I'd like to tell you about a friend of mine in Los Angeles. Late one night, he got a phone call that his son was confined in a mental health clinic in San Francisco. The boy, about 19 years old, had made an unsuccessful attempt at suicide. The psychiatrist on the phone reassured the father that his son was in no physical danger but suggested that a personal interview with the father might be helpful. Could he fly to San Francisco?

When the father arrived the next day, in the late afternoon, the son was angry because the father had "taken so long." He demonstrated his anger by refusing to speak to his father.

When the psychiatrist had them both in his office, he asked the boy why he was giving his father "the silent treatment." The boy told him.

"I see," said the psychiatrist. "So you've made up your mind as to what your father should have done. And you won't settle for any less. You think that a good father—a 100% father—would have taken an earlier plane. So you're discounting him for every hour he was late—by your standards.

"Well, the fact is that he *is* here. So he must care at least a *little*. Maybe 10%? Are you saying that, if you can't have a 100% father, you won't take any less?"

My friend told me later: "I flew up to San Francisco filled with guilt and anger. 'How had I failed my son? How could he do this to me?' But the psychiatrist's question started me thinking. 'Maybe I have been a 10% father. And he's been a 10% son. O.K. I'll try to do better. But starting right now, I'd better accept his 10% instead of rejecting *all* of him because he hasn't entirely lived up to the standards *I've* set for *him*."

It was the start of an understanding between father and son.

People like people who like them. After all, anyone who has such good taste must have other redeeming qualities. And people reward the people they like: with favors, love, promotions, business—everything. But they can't like you unless *you* like you—and them. I'm talking about your *genuinely* admiring that percentage of the whole person—in yourself and others—that you find likeable.

The amazing thing is, that as you re-program your life through Dyna/Psyc, you'll find that everything else, literally, falls into place. One day, very soon, something you are affirming—something you thought was 'impossible''—has happened. You've *made* it happen.

You are indeed the cause of all your effects.

CHAPTER THREE

THE WORLD'S MOST EXCITING BUSINESS

Now I'm going to tell you about the most exciting business in the world. It's just about the last frontier for the "little guy." It's a business you can start in your garage or bedroom, right in your hometown. And, if things go right, you can build a national—even a world-wide—business almost overnight!

It takes very little capital to get started, and if you play your cards right, it's self-financing! You can have thousands of salesmen working for you—some on a straight-commission basis. In other words, you pay them only for what they sell, so your profit is assured.

It's called the Direct Response Business. And probably no other business has so many people who started from scratch and became millionaires. You know some of the giants: Sears-Roebuck, Montgomery-Ward, Spiegel's, and I'm sure you could list a dozen more household names. And there are thousands of less familiar names who are raking in the profits from what Barron's, the financial journal, described as "the fastest growing business in America."

The greatest thing is that you can be, if you pick your spots, on an equal footing with the giants. The discounts they get, through buying power, can be relatively insignificant. And you can more than off-set their advantages by "cutting corners." What's more, because you don't have to filter your profits through layers of people and acres of overhead, you can act more quickly and efficiently.

Here's why the Direct Response Business is growing—and will continue to grow. It offers your customers convenience. It's a lot easier to clip a coupon, make up a check, and stick it in the mailbox than drive to a store, find a parking place, and try to get a clerk's attention.

It's efficient. Most stores have to pay clerks to stand around during the slack hours, just so there'll be enough—or almost enough—to handle the peak periods. In the Direct Response Business, you can spread your workload throughout the day, getting maximum production from every employee.

Customers save by reduced handling costs. The average product has to go through the hands of wholesalers, distributors, and jobbers before it even reaches the retailer. Each one takes his cut—and adds to the cost. And the retailer has to take a good chunk just to cover the cost of prime real estate. To say nothing of a whopping investment in fixtures, and there's the cost of merchandise that's damaged as it's shipped, re-shipped, and shipped again. Those are just a few of the costs that are eliminated or reduced in the Direct Response Business.

And that's why almost anything you can name is sold, using Direct Response methods. And more items are being added every day. Here are some estimates on sales volume—*the number of units sold*—in these categories. The figures are from the trade magazine *Advertising Age:* Kitchen appliances—6,100,000; Tools, under $30—5,200,000; Watches, under $40—2,500,000; Luggage sets, under $30—2,200,000; Tableware sets, under $30—1,600,000; Tools, over $30—1,600,000; Vacuum cleaners—1,200,000; Radios, under $80—1,200,000; Watches, over $40—1,000,000; Cookware sets, under $40—950,000. And those figures do not include sales from catalogs!

Here's more proof that Direct Response is a growing, multi-billion dollar business: Ninety-five of the major corporations listed on the New York Stock Exchange chalk up an important part of their sales, using Direct Response techniques. And some of the biggies—General Foods, General Mills, ITT, and Avon are getting into it.

But don't let the size of the competition scare you off. Because, unlike any other kind of business I can think of, in the case of the Direct Response business, your smallness is an *advantage.* Your direct, personal control and your low overhead work for you. The President of some corporate octopus is not going to go into the business. He's going to have to hire and pay experts, who are going to hire other experts. All in the hope that they'll know what they are doing. And they'll make mistakes—because they're not spending their own money—and never have. They'll have monstrous expenses I'll show you how to avoid. Not the least of which are advertising agencies that take 15% off the top. The discounts that are available in the two most important areas—advertising and mailing costs—are available to *anyone.* In fact, I'll show you how you can pay far less for your advertising than the Big Boys pay *using identical media* (including radio, TV, and newspapers) simply because they are big. What's more, if you mail 200 letters, the Post Office will give you a 40% discount—and that's the *most* you can get, no matter how many more letters you mail! Interestingly, if you mail over 250,000 letters a year, the rate goes up!

Furthermore, in the pages that follow, I'm going to share "trade secrets" that cost me, literally, hundreds of thousands of dollars to discover . . . information that's never been published before.

I believe I've read just about everything that's been written about this business. I can only conclude that the authors didn't know what they were talking about, or didn't know enough, or wouldn't tell what they knew.

As for me, I'm not going to hold anything back. If you follow the procedures I'll outline, step by step, you can have any degree of success you really want: anything from a comfortable "second income" to more money than you ever dreamt was possible.

Why am I willing to do this? Well, because you paid me for it. The ten dollars you sent may be a ridiculously low figure for the value of what you're about to receive. But I think that there are a hundred thousand like you. And ten dollars times a hundred thousand people is one million dollars. So I'll make a lot of money doing what I like best. As for you, you've already had your first—and most important—lesson in the Direct Response Business:

> You can have a lot of fun . . .
> And make a lot of money . . .
> Giving people what they want . . .
> At a reasonable price.

CHAPTER FOUR

TECHNIQUES FOR GETTING UNUSUAL IDEAS

The Direct Response Business can be divided into these 5 major categories: Radio, TV, Newspapers, Magazines, and Direct Mail. But these are really only the means you use to tell people about what you have for sale.

I've used them all successfully. I'll tell you how you can too.

There are other methods of communicating—and making sales—that require *no* investment, and I'll tell you about those too. And what may be the greatest method of making sales is just aborning. It's cable television, and many of the stations are so hungry for business that they'll sell for you on a commission basis. Which means that you'll end up with a small but sure profit.

But the first thing you're going to have to consider—and it's really the hardest part of the problem—is *what* you're going to sell.

The *best* thing to sell is something unique: a better product, a greater service, a lower price. What you're looking for could be any one of these or could include all three. The crucial element is that people should have to come to *you* when they want it.

So first make a list of what you *enjoy* doing and do better than most people. Are you a great cook? Are you a genius at fixing things around the house? Are you a sharp poker player? Does everyone admire the way you refinish furniture? Is there something special you know about attracting people of the opposite sex? When you're on a fishing trip, are you the one who usually ends up with the biggest catch? Are the parties you give the ones that people talk about? Do you get a kick out of meeting new people? Are you the one person in the neighborhood everyone tells his troubles to? Are you the guy people call for advice when they're having trouble with their cars? Are you a whiz at math? Can you make people laugh? Do you know how to butcher a cow? Do people admire your garden? Do you have a good memory?

A million-dollar Direct Response Business has been built on *every one* of these—and there's lots of room for competition!

Start your own list. Use those that are applicable from the examples I've given and add your own. Things you enjoy doing. Things you do better than *most* people. Notice I didn't say "better than anyone." You just have to be better than average. Because if you're just a little better than only half the people in this great country—and they want some skill, product or service that you can do better or more easily than they can—that's a market of one hundred million people! Surely that's enough prospects to start with.

When you've completed your list (and if it's not a long one, work harder on your ISI), try mixing them up to produce an unusual *combination*. For example, if you can make people laugh and you're a great fisherman, you could make a good living as a guest speaker at service club meetings . . . or writing for Field and Stream . . . or printing signs and cards for the tourist trade of fishing resorts . . . or?

Or if butchering a cow and throwing great parties are the two things that really turn you on, maybe you could go into the business of catering barbecues for organizations . . . or you could set up a "party plan" for selling meat wholesale . . . or?

Anyway, you get the point. Fool around with it. Have fun. And keep in mind that you don't have to sell a product. You can sell an idea or a plan; a way to do something better, or faster, or cheaper. There are a lot more people who got rich selling cookbooks than running restaurants. Paper is cheaper than plastic. And people will pay you well for a good idea . . . any idea that will make them healthier or happier or stronger or sexier or richer. Certainly, as you've gone through life, you've learned *something* that other people would like to know . . . and will pay you to find out.

Another way to get ideas is to use Creative Unhappiness. Make notes of the things that bug you: long lines in the supermarket, a gadget that won't work, surly waiters, paperback books that are printed too close to the margin, cluttered TV commercials, the kids leaving the lights on in every room of the house, your spouse snoring, cleaning up after the dog, dripping faucets.

Remember that the things that annoy you bother other people too. And, if you can find a way to get rid of some petty annoyance, people will be glad to pay you for your solution.

Turn Worry into Wampum! If you have a serious problem, attack it. Don't just let it whirl round and round in your head, making you miserable and robbing you of sleep. Look at it as a challenge—an opportunity—because it is. When you figure out the answer, you could have a profitable business on your hands.

Let me give you an example:

When I was head over heels in debt, I knew that there were two things I could do: (1) Declare bankruptcy or (2) Work my way out. The first alternative would be a "legal" solution to my problem. But, in my eyes, it would not be an honorable one. My creditors had "loaned" me money in good faith. If I didn't pay them back, I would be betraying that faith. I'd given my word and I wouldn't break it. It was as simple as that.

But I also had an obligation to my family—to house, clothe, and feed them decently. Not luxuriously—just decently. So, obviously, any repayment program would have to take that primary obligation into account. It had to be something we could live with—and for a long time, because a $50,000 debt wouldn't be repaid overnight. (It took us 8 years).

So I started to find out everything I could about getting out of debt. I interviewed four lawyers and a judge to find out what my legal rights were: what my creditors could and couldn't do.

My wife and I inventoried the material things we had and the qualities of our life that were essential to us as individuals and a family. We decided which were important to us and which we could do without. We discovered, of course, that the things that were truly meaningful to us—the beach, the parks, the forests, the museums, reading, the picnics, and good conversation, for example—were all free. The other things we enjoyed—an occasional evening at the theatre, a dinner out—could be budgeted and the pleasure actually enhanced. It was *more* fun to find "bargains" in these areas: the rundown movie houses where you could see two good features for 50 cents; the off-beat store-front restaurants where you could get an excellent meal for less than two dollars. (Someday I'm going to write a book "The Gourmet's Guide to Budget Restaurants." There are hundreds of them in every large city. Why don't you write one for *your* town?)

As we compiled our list of all the things we had to have—including shelter, utilities, furniture, food, transportation, clothing, medical and dental bills, etc.—we researched how to get the most for our money. Incidentally, Christmas is not an "Emergency." It happens every year and has to be saved for—in advance.

When we finished our list of essentials, we made up a budget, allotting the necessary money for each thing, including an Emergency Fund, a Savings Fund, and one called "We're Just Human Beings." The last was a small amount set aside so we could buy or do something "foolish" (and human) once in awhile.

Then we made up envelopes for each category and put the necessary cash in an envelope every week. There are two important elements in that preceding sentence: "Cash" and "every week." "Cash" because you can see it and touch it. It's *real*—and much easier to keep track of than a bank balance. "Every week" because when you provide for your monthly payments on this basis, it's a lot easier than having to come up with a lump—and 4-1/3 times larger—sum at the end of the month.

The rules we set up were: (1) You couldn't "borrow" from one envelope if you developed a shortage in another. (2) If you had an overage, it had to go into the Emergency Fund or the Savings Fund. (3) We bought nothing on credit.

Because when you buy on credit, you usually can't make as good a "buy" and you have to pay for the money you're borrowing. That meant we had to *anticipate* our needs for major purchases and/or repairs—furniture, appliances, a car, whatever—and budget for them in advance so we'd have the money when we needed it . . . by setting it aside every week.

Each of the kids had his own envelopes. For "School Expenses," for example. For "Snacks" (this kept us from being "nickeled and dimed" to death). For "Clothing" (this kept us from being nagged for the faddish clothes that "all of the other kids" had. If they really wanted it, they could buy it—and figure out what they were going to do without.)

The pleasantest byproduct of all this planning was that it brought us closer together as a family. The kids actually felt more secure, more a part of the action. And we think they learned valuable lessons about money—where it comes from and where it goes. All of us got more pleasure from the things our money bought because we were in *control*. We didn't have to make dozens of little decisions every day.

Could we—or couldn't we—afford this or that? We could afford anything we really wanted as long as there was enough money in the envelope—and we had decided what we could do without. In simple terms, we could have steak for dinner any day of the week . . . but it would mean some corner-cutting on the other 6 days . . . and, occasionally, it was worth it.

The Budget Plan eliminated most of our careless "impulse buying." In other words, it stopped us from buying a lot of things we didn't really want or need. We didn't just "buy" things; we *shopped* for them. And it was *fun*—pitting our skills against a whole world of businessmen who were bombarding us with advertising, sometimes trying to mislead or cheat us, always anxious to separate us from our money.

I found out that setting up a Budget Plan and making it work is crucial. Dun and Bradstreet, the credit reporting firm, says that over 90% of all businesses fail within 5 years after they've opened their doors. Most of these failures have one thing in common: they don't keep good records. And, without records, they don't know what they're doing . . . where they've been, where they are, or where they're going. I think that most family finances fail or stay in hot water for the same reason.

These are some of the other things about getting out of debt, staying out of debt, and having more money to spend that my research uncovered:

How you can make yourself judgment and attachment-proof!

How you can have thousands of dollars in assets that creditors can't touch!

How to use the little-known Law of Debt Relief to protect what you have (your home, car, salary, possessions) from grasping creditors!

How to pay off debts—on *your* terms!

How to *avoid* bankruptcy—by *preparing* for it!

Why there are certain old bills you'd better *not* pay—or even acknowledge!

Why not owing *enough* money can be worse than owing too much!

How to beat a greedy merchant out of excessive interest charges—and even collect damages!

Where to get *free* legal advice!

How to win a lawsuit!

Which creditors to pay *first.* (The ones who are bullying you probably have the least chance of collecting!)

How "going bankrupt" can actually *improve* yor credit rating!

Where you can legally deposit your savings so they're probably safe, even if you do go bankrupt!

How and where to borrow at "wholesale" rates!

How to get your hands on money you may not know you have!

All of these things, and a lot more, are perfectly legal—*and* honorable. They are based on laws and facts that the Easy Credit Merchants, Finance Companies, and the Collection Agencies hope you won't find out about. But an honest man can use this information to pay off his bills in an orderly fashion without living in fear or being sick with worry.

Which brings us back to the original point: How to turn Worry into Wampum. When I'd worked out a plan for getting us out of debt, I realized that there had to be a lot of people in the same boat. So I wrote a book titled "The Power of Money Management."* I then wrote an ad, headlined "Get out of debt in 90 minutes—without borrowing!" (The 90 minutes referred to the legal steps you can take, with or without a lawyer, that stop creditors from badgering you.)

Some newspapers and magazines refused to publish the ad. (The Easy Credit Merchants and Finance Companies are big advertisers.) The Bar Association investigated the ad and the book—and cleared both . . . somewhat reluctantly. (After all, lawyers have to make a living too.)

* © 1967, Financial Publishers, 466 North Western Avenue, Los Angeles, CA 9000∠

The net result was that I sold over 100,000 copies at $3.95 each.

In solving my own problems—and sharing the solution—I made a lot of money and, not so incidentally, helped a lot of other people with debt problems.

So I'm going to hand you a great opportunity. Make a list of your worries. Pick your biggest, meanest Worry. Then make a list of alternatives . . . the ways the problem might be solved. Next, gather all the information you can about the possible solutions. Usually, at this point, the answer will be obvious. If it's not, or if you don't like the answer, simply turn the problem over to your Unconscious Computer.

When you get your solution—and you will—you could be on your way to getting rich! First, because you'll have proved to yourself how easily you can rid yourself of your own worries. Second, if it was a really Big Worry—one that a lot of other people share—they'll be glad to pay you for telling them how to solve it.

Turn Worry into Wampum!

If you don't have any worries of your own, here's a list of things that other people are concerned about. They represent a compilation of the questions (almost 300,000 last year) sent into the research division of the Encyclopaedia Brittanica. The list is in order of highest interest (the greatest number of questions):

Careers, Buying a house, Starting a small business, Family budgets, ESP and the occult, Building own home, Winemaking at home, Camping, Reading speed improvement.

Memory improvement, Tropical fish, Furniture finishing and refinishing, Basic drawing and sketching, Extra-biblical evidence of the existence of Jesus.

Environmental pollution, Zero population growth, World energy and natural resources, Drugs, narcotics and related problems, Conditions in China, Possibilities of future trade with Russia and China, Monetary problems related to devaluation, Arab-Israeli conflicts, Northern Ireland crisis, Conditions of Jews in Russia, Canadian separatist movement, Consumerism, Prison reform, Gun control, National Health Insurance, Amnesty for draft dodgers.

Public welfare, Crime problems, Wage and price controls, Civil rights, Education—finance, busing, child-care centers, open classroom concepts, Computer-assisted education, pre-school and mentally retarded.

Chess strategies, Life in outer space and UFOs, Scientific questions about quasars, pulsars, continental drift, Biofeedback, brain wave control, Biological rhythms, Freezing the dead, Property taxes.

That's what other people are worrying about. I think it's obvious that millions of dollars are already being made, providing some of the answers. But I assure you that they haven't scratched the surface. So go to it—pick a worry you really like—and get rich!

When you're problem-solving, don't overlook the obvious. The best answers are usually brilliantly simple. Don't fret that "It's so obvious that someone else must have thought of it," with the inference that "It's so easy; something must be wrong with it." Chances are that someone else *did* think of it . . . and abandoned the idea for that very reason. Don't make the same mistake.

Let me tell you about a modest, personal experience with the danger of overlooking the obvious.

When I got out of the Service in 1945, I was 20 years old, married, had one child. I went over to UCLA to enroll and saw the long lines of students queuing up in front of the Registrar's window. I decided that 2 years, 9 months and 13 days of waiting in line for food, crew-haircuts, supplies, and the latrine had been enough. I wasn't going to wait in line for an education. I was going to get a job.

But I found out there wasn't really a big demand for ex-third class Pharmacist's Mates with a high school degree. The only job I was offered at what we called the 52-20 Club (because, for 52 weeks an unemployed veteran could draw up to $20 a week) was as a Roller Skate Assembler. It paid $35 a week for a 48-hour week. When I turned it down, the 52-20 man told me that I was ungrateful and cut off the $20 a week.

Now I was not only ungrateful, I was broke. And I was mad. For years, an older friend of mine had been telling me about all the money that could be made in the surplus business. Not War Surplus, but the surplus goods acquired by manufacturers and businesses. Things they'd sell cheap because they couldn't dispose of them through their normal channels. You didn't have to have any capital, he said, because you didn't buy anything until you had a customer.

Well, I was scared—but desperate. So I took a streetcar into downtown Los Angeles. The first big building I saw was the May Company Department Store. I want up to their Purchasing Office. I told the lady that I was in the Surplus Business—did they have anything they wanted to sell? She thought for a moment, then said there was one thing. The May Company had about 20,000 small cardboard shipping cartons. It seemed that during World War II, the government had specified that all packages sent overseas to servicemen had to be shipped in this kind of a carton. Now, with the war over, nobody was buying them. Would I like to make her an offer?

I swallowed hard and told her I would have to call my "associate," who was our company expert on shipping cartons. In a daze, I wandered out of her office and into a phone booth. I held the phone book dumbly in my hands. Who would want to buy 20,000 shipping cartons that weren't being used to mail packages overseas any more? The only obvious answer was a "paper jobber" who would sell them to small manufacturing companies for their shipping needs. But surely the Purchasing Office Lady would have thought of this outlet. It was too simple. There must be some reason the paper jobbers couldn't use them.

But, out of sheer desperation, I looked in the Yellow Pages and found the largest ad. (It turned out later to be a very small company.) Sure enough, a line in the ad assured me that they bought and sold cardboard cartons. I called them, described the carton the best I could, and asked what they'd pay for 20,000. The man told me 1½¢ a piece—$300 for the lot. I thanked him and told him I'd let him know.

I went back to the Purchasing Office and told the lady I'd pay her $250. She accepted the offer. I was in the Surplus Business, and I had made $50 the very first day—the equivalent of a week and a half's pay as a Roller Skate Assembler!

Most important, I'd learned my lesson: Never Overlook the Obvious. Sure, the Purchasing Office lady could have made the same phone call. But she had a lot of other things on her mind—and it wasn't her money. But I was concentrating on that one little problem—and it was *my* money if I could solve it.

I did find out later that the boxes were really worth at "wholesale," about a nickel a piece or $1000 for the lot—and about $2000 at "retail." And that they were easily saleable because there was a paper shortage. But no matter, my business career was launched, and I'd learned a lesson that would profit me a thousandfold.

The windup on this story is that in less than 6 months, we moved out of my in-law's house into a handsome apartment, paid cash for a brand-new car, and had $10,000 in the bank. All because it occurred to me that if the May Company had a large inventory of these "obsolete" boxes, the same must be true of every major department store and dime store in the country. I didn't have the capital, so I had to buy one batch, sell it, and then parlay the profits to buy a bigger batch. Storage space was scarce and expensive so I rented private garages in my neighborhood for 3 to 5 dollars a month. It was slow and a lot of hard work. But it sure beat assembling roller skates!

Incidentally, there's still a lot of money to be made in the Surplus Business. Is it something you'd enjoy doing? The only basic it requires is imagination.

Imagination is the key to all success. Which brings us to the next point. It's the counter-point to "Don't overlook the obvious." This lesson is entitled "Don't accept the obvious."

To illustrate, I'm going to ask you to change the following figure into a "6," using only a single line:

Work on it before you turn the page for the answer.

Here's the answer:

SIX

Simple wasn't it? But only one out of 500 will get it right. The "trick" is that most people immediately see the "ix" as a Roman numeral, and they're trapped. Or they think only in terms of a straight line, not a curved one. They accept what is "obvious."

In trying to find an imaginative solution to a problem, examine what "everybody else" is doing. Don't assume that, with their wider experience "they" must be right. They may just be playing "follow the leader." Instead, apply what I call "Operation Zig-Zag." Determine what everyone else is doing—and then ask yourself what would happen if you did just the opposite—when "they" zig, *you* zag.

Successful restaurant businesses have been built by advertising "Lousy food, bad service" or something to that effect. True, nobody believed the sign or they just had to find out for themselves. But it worked. It got people to try the food and service—at least once.

When I started advertising for the Ford agency I mentioned earlier, we looked at what our competitors were doing. You can tell me what it was, because they're still doing it. Everyone was the largest, offered the best trade-ins, practically gave cars away, and if you didn't have enough money to buy a car, they'd loan it to you. On TV, they always sponsored old movies so they could have frequent, long commercials, and show lots of their used car "bargains."

They did all this because that was the way it had "always been done," and the techniques had apparently worked very well for some of the car dealers. (Happily, most of the competitors we surveyed at that time have since gone broke. In fact, all except one—which only proves that you can't lose 'em all.)

So how do you go about advertising for a small car dealer, in an inconvenient location, who has a few green salesmen?

Well, when all else fails, tell the truth (it works wonders in advertising). In our advertising, we told people that we were a small car dealer in an inconvenient location, with a few green salesmen. Then we also admitted that we were in business to make a profit—at least enough so that we could be around long enough to give them the service they had coming. We didn't show any used cars or quote any "bargain" prices. We shared our feeling that if a car was priced way below the market, it must be because that was all the car was really worth or the dealer was losing money . . .

and why would a dealer add the cost of advertising to the loss he was already taking on a sale—unless he really didn't intend to sell it?

We interviewed lots of customers ("live" so we couldn't be accused of editing) who told how they'd saved money or had a financing problem solved. We guaranteed that we'd do anything within reason—and a few things that were unreasonable—to keep a customer happy.

Instead of having a lot of long commercials in one movie, we bought a lot of comparatively short commercials in many different kinds of programs.

In other words, where our competitors zigged, we zagged. The whole campaign was directed towards building confidence and believability, because we thought that people distrusted car dealers in general. And you have to be trusted if you're going to sell something to anyone. And you have to live up to that trust if you're going to sell them again.

The result: The Ford agency netted over a million dollars in the first 3 years. Moral: Don't accept the obvious.

There are two reasons why you should *welcome* problems:

1. As you solve them, you rebuild your self-image. It's powerful help in correcting your ISI. And the knowledge, the skill, the practice in problem-solving you gain as you solve each problem makes it easier to solve the next one!
2. When you solve a really BIG problem, in an imaginative way, you could be laying the foundation for an exciting, enriching business.

Problem-solving is an *adventure*. It'll take you places you've never been before. It'll make you *see* things you've only *looked* at before. One of the curious things that happens when you start researching your answers is what I call "Tuning In."

"Tuning in" works like this: When you get interested in a subject, you "tune in" sources of information you would have otherwise missed. Articles in newspapers and magazines, TV and radio programs, the conversations of friends, the sermon at church—all of these things and more—suddenly start coming into your awareness. You get vital input you would not have seen or heard if you hadn't been "tuned in."

In my own case, I'm not sure whether the information was there all along and I had missed it—or whether some kind of magnetism I've unleashed is drawing the new material and attracting people who can help to me. It doesn't matter. It works.

When you're tracking down answers, do it with energy and enthusiasm. Don't be afraid to ask questions. No one will think you're stupid. Remember that Will Rogers, the Cowboy Philosopher, said: "We're *all* ignorant . . . only on different subjects." Experts are flattered by your interest in "their" subject.

Don't be afraid to make a mistake.

When you make a mistake, make it a WHOPPER! Anyone can make a careless or thoughtless mistake. All that shows is that you weren't paying attention—or weren't interested.

But a BIG mistake . . . one that you've put a lot of thought, heart and sweat into . . . a mistake that you made after carefully weighing the alternatives and energetically implementing the conclusions—now, *that's* a mistake to be proud of!

Babe Ruth held two records: one for home runs—and the other for strike-outs. But he isn't remembered for his strike-outs.

I don't know of any advance in science that was made without a whole series of mistakes being made. And what's "science" but a systematized approach to solving problems? *Each "failure" brings you one step closer to the right answer!*

I know one insurance salesman who used the phone to "prospect." He figured out that for every ten "cold calls" he made, he got 9 "No's" and 1 "Yes." So each "No" was not a rebuff, It was just a step up the ladder. He could hardly wait to go up the nine steps so he could get what he was after—the "Yes" at the top!

My only question iş: could he, with Dyna/Psyc, have *raised* his expectations—say one "Yes" for every five "No's"?

A few years ago I helped set up a sales training program for real estate salesmen. Through interviews with the most successful salesmen, we had been able to determine what they did to find prospects, make presentations, close sales.

We distilled the best techniques and taught them to the new salesmen. This was a Formula for Success. Because we were able to prove to them if they followed our program, step-by-step, that they would get the following results:

For every five phone calls they made, they would make one appointment. Two out of three people would keep the appointment and one would cancel. One out of three of the people who kept the appointment would visit the property being sold. And one out of three who visited the property would buy. So all the new salesmen had to do is make 15 phone calls to wind up with one sale. And since the average commission was $850, that made *each* phone call—whether the particular answer was "Yes" or "No"—worth $56.66! If they made 30 phone calls a day, worked five days a week, took a two-week vacation, their income for the year would be $42,495!

Success is a matter of viewpoint. The pessimist sees the bottle as half-empty. The optimist sees it as half-full.

My wife is the most optimistic person I know. I tease her that if she found a pile of manure in the middle of the living room, she'd clap her hands and say "Oh boy! Somebody gave me a pony!"

She bounces out of bed each morning, eager to discover the delightful surprises she knows the day holds.

She knows that everyone loves her and that they delight in her enthusiasm and curiosity. If, infrequently, she meets someone who isn't taken with her charm, she's disturbed, at most, only momentarily. She wonders (if she reacts to it at all) what's wrong with *them*.

You may wonder why I dwell so much on salesmen. Because we're all salesmen. When you were a "helpless" infant, you had to occasionally convince your mother that you needed to be fed. When you were a child and growing up you had to use sales techniques on your parents to get what you wanted. You had to "sell" yourself to your lover, your boss, your customers, your friends. The technique was always the same. All you had to show them was that you had something *they* wanted . . . even if it was "only" your respect or admiration . . . even if it was only the self-respect they achieved by doing their duty.

So we're *all* salesmen—good, bad and indifferent. And the good salesmen *get* more because they *expect* more.

Don't be afraid to ask "Why?"

It's no accident that children learn most during their first six years . . . before we start "educating" them and getting them to memorize "facts" instead of youthfully pursuing their interests and satisfying their curiosity.

The two subjects our schools teach best are "Sitting Still" and "Being Quiet." A child can "pass" if he does very little else. Then we wonder why adults are so passive. Why they have so little energy (call it ambition or "get up and go"). Why they accept the "rules" without question.

That's because they've learned their lesson—"that's how you get along"—and they've learned it well.

Well, don't just "get along"—Get Ahead!

The person who asks "Why?" shows that he's not just "doing"—he's *thinking*. And he'll probably find a *better* way to do it. Business is hungry for Thinkers. They'll shower them with rewards because there are so few Thinkers. Lots of doers but very few Thinkers. And all you have to do to be a Thinker is use the magic word. It's "Why?"

Don't be afraid to take chances!

How many people do you know who have starved to death? You won't starve either.

When you've figured out where you want to go—jump! If there's a two foot chasm between where you are and the next peak, the only way you'll fall in is by taking a timid step.

My father-in-law, who's in his late seventies, told me something I never forgot. I was a little nervous about having bought our new home. I thought I could swing the payments, but what if . . .

He said, "What's the worst that could happen? You might live in your beautiful new house for a couple of years and then lose it. But you'll have had it for a couple of years, and you can *never* lose that *memory*. Isn't that better than never having had it at all?" He paused for a moment, and I could sense that he was looking back on his own life. "You know," he said quietly, "the only things I regret . . . are the things I didn't do."

Set aside a definite, prescribed time each day to build your new life. Include your Daily Declarations in the morning when you get up and just before you go to sleep. Time: 20 minutes. Super-Suggestion once each day. Time: 10 minutes. Then take a half-hour, an hour—whatever you can spare—to make your Goals a reality. RSVP—Read! Study! Visualize! Perform!

That's an average of an hour and a half out of your 16 waking hours— 9 per cent—to discover what *you* have that *other* people want. And that 9% of your time is probably time that you're frittering away worrying or watching TV or something else that's meaningless. But 9% of your Life is 7 years! And even if you've lived more than half of it, that's 3 years. Can you think of many problems that couldn't be solved in *three years* of concentrated effort?

So don't tell me you "haven't got the time." The wisest man I ever knew told me that "Most people are too busy earning a living to make any money." Don't take as long as I did to find out he was right.

Every newspaper and magazine is crammed with Business Opportunities—and I don't mean the ads or the ones that appear in the Classified Section. Newspapers and magazines report the things that people are interested in and concerned about. Today. Right now.

Here are one day's headlines and some rather obvious products they suggest—most of which could be or are being sold by Direct Response methods.

"Unruh Urges Free Rides for Elderly"

The Senior Citizens have millions of dollars to spend for leisure, gifts for their grandchildren. They're concerned about property taxes, hospitalization costs. How can you help them?

"Sued Firm Agrees to Cancel Subscriptions"

How about a consumer newsletter warning people in your town about rackets?

"8 Day Gospel Convention to be Held Here"

Conventioneers need places to stay and places to go, souveniers.

"Family of Gang-War Victim Makes Appeal"

So much violence. What about a personal alarm that people could carry?

"Gas Credit Card Fees Deductible"

How about a pamphlet listing over-looked deductions?

"Panel Says Autos Can Meet 1975 Smog Goal"

How about lightweight gas-masks that people can wear til 1975? More serious answer: Natural gas is a practically smogless fuel. It triples engine life and the "life" of your oil and lube jobs. Its only drawbacks are that a car loses about 10% in speed of acceleration and you can only go about 120 miles on a tankful. So who needs to go from 0 to 60 in 10 seconds?—Nine seconds is fast enough for me. And, there are dual-fuel systems available for about $500, installed. So you could still go on long trips, using the natural gas for the trips around town that rack up 90% of your mileage. Mileage figures are about the same, and natural gas costs about 7 cents a gallon! (It's apparent that I've done some research on this. But I'm not greedy. C'mon in; the money's fine!)

"Traffic Snarled as Drifting Snow Covers Midwest"

Could roads be heated like an electric blanket by "planting" wires when they're paved—and melt the snow?

"48 Meat Plants Called Unclean in '72"

Could you start a maintenance service to take care of this problem for them?

So much for the news. When I look over the ads, I really can't see a thing that couldn't be sold better and cheaper by Direct Response. Even cars are being sold that way, and I'm told that a buyer can save several hundred dollars.

I've told you a few of the ways that you can develop a unique product or service. Probably the best ones will crop up when you open up your mind to the possibilities.

For example:

1. We were testing some "invisible" powders that would help trap thieves. That didn't work out the way we hoped. But we suddenly realized that a process we'd developed would make it possible to produce Christmas ornaments that would be shatterproof, glow in the dark, and sell for a little more than 5 cents apiece (6 dozen for $4). We've sold millions and are selling more every year.

2. I was talking to my best friend. I found out that he had a manuscript telling all about "How to Build Your Own Swimming Pool for Less Then $500."* I arranged to have it published. The books cost us about 50 cents and we sold them for $10. The people who bought them got more than their money's worth—and we made out all right.

3. One of the newspaper sales representatives who called on me kidded me about what an easy way I had of making a living. He said that he'd like to find something to sell—and get away from punching a clock. I asked him what he liked to do best. He grinned and told me, "Play the horses." I asked him if he was any good at it; he told me "Yes." So I suggested that he write a book. I needled him for about 2 years, but he never did write the book. But he did run into a guy named Larry Voegele, who had a fantastic record of success at picking the winners—and *had* written a book "Professional Method of Winner Selection"† I bought the rights, and last year we sold 72,000 copies at $10 apiece . . . and it's still going strong.

   The former newspaper sales representative quit his job and became my associate in a Handicapping School. At the Handicapping School, Larry Voegele (The Master) teaches what he knows in a 3 night course that costs $200. The fellow who introduced us is the Administrator and probably makes more money working from 9 to noon than he did when he was peddling space full time—and has plenty of time to go to the track.

4. My wife read a newspaper article about a new kind of diet plan developed by a doctor. We investigated and saw the possibilities

---

* © 1972, Financial Publishers, 466 North Western Avenue, Los Angeles, CA 90004
† © 1968, Financial Publishers, 466 North Western Avenue, Los Angeles, CA 90004

of marketing it. The circulation of that newspaper is over a million. But one person who read that article, *did* something about it. The result: the Northwestern Weight-Loss Plan is now the largest selling product in its field.

5. A client of mine gave me about 200 door-viewers. (You know the things they put in doors, so the person inside can see who's outside without being seen.) He'd imported about 500 from Germany; these were the remains and he couldn't seem to sell them. He thought maybe I could figure out what to do with them. At any rate, we moved them out of his warehouse into mine. There, they gathered dust for 2 years.

One day the shipping clerk told me they were in the way and asked if he should throw them out. Well, I was too cheap to do that, so I called a wholesale hardware company and a couple of retail hardware stores. They all gave me the same story. They weren't interested in an odd lot of what was, at best, a slow moving item. They already had regular suppliers of "name brand" merchandise. The challenge nagged me, and I finally assigned the problem to my Unconscious Computer. A few days later, driving home, I got the answer.

Why should a door viewer be installed in just a front door? Why not *any* door? Or in a fence? Or even a wall?

So I pulled off the freeway, into a gas station. I scribbled out an ad. I can't say I "wrote" it. It just came to me. (That's one of the creepy things that happens when you use your Unconscious Computer.)

The headline was "Super-Spy Lets You See Through Walls, Fences, and Locked Doors!" The ad resulted in interviews on national radio and TV; was reprinted by a Los Angeles Times columnist (who hated it) and by New Yorker Magazine (who thought it was funny). Most important, it sold over 140,000 door viewers—so far.

Don't get me wrong. I've had my share of flops. Can you figure out what to do with a game that tests your ESP Quotient? Or a book called "Formula for Youth"? Or some beautiful Christmas cards with a sculptured medallion that glows in the dark?

We sold some of these items, but not enough to make it interesting. But someday . . .

The secret of success in this business (or maybe any business) is to milk your winners—and when you lay an egg, cut your losses. If you've taken your best shot, and it hasn't worked, forget it and go on to the next project. Since you can test your potential so inexpensively (and I'll show you how) you can have an awful lot of losers before you can have one winner. And the Winner will make up your losses—and then some.

Here are some more ways to develop a product or service: When looking at something, play "What Would Happen If."

What Would Happen If . . .

It was larger?

It was smaller?

It was upside down?

It was inside out?

You charged more?

You charged less?

You used it in a different way?

It was made out of a better kind of material?

It was made out of a cheaper kind of material?

S-t-r-e-t-c-h your imagination! It's a muscle and develops with use.

I've told you a lot of different ways you can find a product or service to sell.

Now I'm going to warn you about a couple of things I do *not* recommend:

1. Don't become a "distributor" for some gadget unless you get an *exclusive* from the manufacturer. Even if you do, be careful. Just the other night, a magazine sales representative told me this true story:

   A small businessman had a modest success selling a wooden chest for coasters for $7.95. A larger firm noticed that the ads were repeated and deduced that it was a success. So he played "What Would Happen If" it was made of a *simulated* wood and offered it for $4.95. Then a larger firm played the same game, produced it out of plastic and sold it for $2.95. Recently, a very large firm produced the same item in a very cheap styro-foam and is selling it for $1.49!

   Don't be too reassured if the gadget is patented. There are plenty of unscrupulous people who know that patents don't hold up or can be changed slightly. In any event, patent litigation is very costly and it takes a long, long time to get to court.

2. Don't fall for "Mail Order Courses" or "Get Into the Import Business; Buy at Wholesale" approach. Mostly for the reasons I've already enumerated (lack of exclusivity, etc.). But, even more important, because you'll be paying too much for the

merchandise. (I'll go into that at greater length later.) Most of these outfits are primarily interested in charging you for having your firm name printed on a catalog. Then you have to dig up the mailing list (more about *that* later too) and pay the postage costs. Any orders that do straggle in result in a *sure* profit for them . . . and a doubtful one for you.

Besides, if you *use* the techniques I've described, you can come up with enough products of your own. And that's the best—and most profitable—kind.

There are opportunities all around—and within—you.
> First, *Make Up* Your Mind—to make money!
> Second, *Change* You Mind—with Dyna/Psyc!
> Third, *Open* Your Mind—so you can truly see what you've only "looked at" before.

CHAPTER FIVE

PRICING AND BUSINESS PRACTICES

The most common (and usually fatal) mistake that the amateur in the Direct Response Business makes is in the area of Pricing.

He simply doesn't realize how much he has to charge in order to make a profit.

The inflexible rule is this: Your selling price must be at least three times your actual cost.

"Actual cost" is defined as:

1. The cost of the product,
2. The cost of packaging (materials and labor),
3. The cost of postage.

For example, if you're going to sell a Widget, and the actual total cost is one dollar, your sales price must be a minimum of three dollars.

Now using that minimum as a base, how much can you charge for it without running into buyer resistance? That depends of course on the item. What do similar or competitive products cost? What's it readily worth to a buyer in terms of what it'll do for him or save him? How important is the problem that your Widget solves?

The price you want to charge is the one that will give you the best return on your investment. And the best way to determine that optimum price is by testing.

Let's say that you're undecided whether to charge three, four or five dollars. To test, you prepare ads that are identical in every detail, except one—the price.

Then, for this purpose, you divide your prospects into three parts. Let's say that you are going to mail 3,000 letters to people who should be interested in what you're selling. (I say 3,000 because the larger the "sample," the more you can rely on the results.) What you would do is mail a thousand letters offering the $3 price; a thousand letters quoting the $4 price; and another thousand giving the $5 price.

Be sure that the *only* difference between the letters is the price and that they're *all* mailed at the same time. That's because *when* a person receives a letter can have a strong influence on whether they respond to it or not. Furthermore, when you're testing, be sure that the different offers are *equally distributed* if there's an economic differential in the areas you're mailing to.

When you get the orders, tabulate the results. The price offer that produced the greatest number of dollars is the one you'll probably want to use from then on. (There's another factor to weigh, which I'll go into at the end of this chapter.) However, if the difference in response is less than 5%, you usually go with the lower price.

For example, let's suppose you get a hundred orders at three dollars ($300); ninety orders at $4 ($360); and 74 orders at $5 ($370). The price you'd set would be $4. First, because the difference between dollar returns on the $4 offer and $5 offer is statistically insignificant. (Statisticians tell us that you have to allow for a 5% "error.") Second, your $4 offer produced almost 18% more customers. And those names are *valuable*—for your own use to mail similar or related offers in the future; to rent to other people in the Direct Response Business. In fact, there are many firms in this business who get the *major* portion of their income from renting their customer lists to firms with non-competitive offers.

I said the names were valuable, and I'll prove it. We have one highly specialized list of about 75,000. I turned down an offer of a dollar per name on an outright sale! Why? Because I expect to make more than that this year alone, just "renting" the names—and I'll still own them.

Back to Pricing. What do you do if you can't get a minimum of three times your actual cost? I can tell you the answer in two words: Forget it. And go on to something else.

Now the 3 to 1 markup doesn't *assure* you of success. It just gives you a fighting chance. I'm simply stating, flatly, that you have no possibility of succeeding without it.

Are there *any* exceptions? Yes—one. When you're handling a high-priced item and the number of dollars of *profit* generated by each sale is sufficient. What do I mean by "sufficient"? Let's say that you're selling a refrigerator by mail for $200 (assuming that that's a bargain price). Furthermore, let's assume that the manufacturers will absorb all of the delivery, installation, service and warranty costs. In that case, your only "product" costs are your overhead (including rent, phone, utilities, insurance, etc.), salaries for people to write up and process the orders. And let's say that all that comes to $500 a month.

If the manufacturer is paying you $20 for each sale, you'd have to sell at least 75 refrigerators a month for a gross profit of $1500 before you could hope to make a modest profit.

So the exception isn't really an exception at all. You still have to have at least that bare-bones minimum mark-up of 3 to 1 ($1500 income for $500 of actual cost!)

And if you have to stock any of the refrigerators or perform any of the services that the Theoretical Manufacturing Company was absorbing in our example, those added costs have become part of *your* "product" cost . . . and you have to get that same 3 to 1 mark-up on those added costs as well.

Incidentally, if you thought that the idea of selling refrigerators by mail was outlandish, remember that 6,100,000 kitchen appliances were sold by mail last year . . . *not* including catalog sales. And Sears, Montgomery-Ward and Spiegel's, and the hundreds of discount catalog operations, sold quite a few more.

If you think that a 3 to 1 mark-up is exorbitant, let me point out a few facts:

The average manufacturer figures the retail price will have to be at least five times his manufacturing cost. If he doesn't, he'll go bankrupt just as sure as accountants use red ink.

The Brand Name vitamins that the manufacturer recommends you take once a day sell at $2.95 for a bottle of 100. I buy the identical product for 29 cents—and the man I buy them from makes a profit.

The finest lipstick that money can buy costs the manufacturer less than two cents. The case costs anywhere from two cents to as much as a dime, if it's really fancy. Check the retail prices of lipstick at the Dime Stores and the hoity-toity Department Stores.

In fact, almost every pharmaceutical or cosmetic manufacturer knows his product has to sell for 10 times—or as much as 20 times—his cost. Does that mean that all the pharmaceutical and cosmetic manufacturers who do provide for this price structure get rich? No, just a few of them. The others quit or go broke.

If you have a Widget that retails for a dollar and you want to sell it to a chain of Auto Supply Stores or Discount Drug Stores, here's what you'll have to face (if they agree to buy your Widget at all): They'll pay you thirty cents *if* you agree to pay the shipping costs, pay for the advertising, agree to take back any Widgets that the customers return, and sell your Widgets on what they call "On Consignment" or "Pay on Reorder." That means that they'll pay you when and if they sell the Widgets and will return the ones that are unsold.

Recently I read that Eastman Kodak gets a 6 to 1 mark-up on its film. And do you have any idea of the actual product cost of toothpaste, mouthwash, cigarettes, cereal, or laundry products? It's *pennies*.

The only time that a major store will operate on less than a 3 to 1 mark-up is when the merchandise is so highly advertised that they feel they *have* to stock it. Or it's a high-priced or "Big Ticket" item with enough profit-dollars to make it worthwhile. Or they want to use if for a "loss-leader." And with all this apparent profit-gouging, most of the successful businessmen in this country end up with a net profit of a little more than five per cent!

Now do you feel better? Do you see why that minimum 3 to 1 mark-up is not only "in line"—but necessary?

Unfortunately, it's not really enough. It's *only* a minimum, only the rock-bottom kind of mark-up you *have* to have *before* you decide to try selling something.

Personally, I feel much more comfortable with 5 to 1. And with 10 to 1, I haven't got a sure thing, but the odds are sure on my side!

Why do I—and you—need as much mark-up as we can reasonably get?

First, so we can afford to make mistakes. Show me a man that doesn't make a mistake, and I'll show you a man who isn't *doing* anything. In this business, as in any business, you have to keep trying: new products, new approaches, new media. And you can't do that unless you can afford to be wrong. The richest rewards go to the people who aren't afraid to take a chance. Even the turtle knows that he can't get ahead unless he sticks his neck out.

The second reason that we need the 10 to 1 mark-up if the product merits it, is so that we can afford to spend a lot of money on advertising. So we can sell more product. So we can make more money. But if you lowered the price, wouldn't you sell more? Not necessarily. Sometimes the public equates quality with price. They feel that if it's too cheap that it can't be any good. Want to find out? Test your prices in the way I outlined at the beginning of the chapter. The public will tell you how much—or how little—they're willing to pay. All you have to do is ask them. And when they tell you what your product's worth, you'd better pay attention.

How much do I budget for Advertising? I go into a deal prepared to spend 50% on advertising—50 cents out of every dollar that comes in. Now my actual advertising may cost me a lot less. I've spent as little as 3%—and as much as 300%. In other words, I've had some cases where a $5 order cost me 15 cents in advertising cost, and I've had other cases where every $5 order cost me $15. One offsets the other (hopefully), and the average is about 50%. The advertising cost to get a $5 order is $2.50.

That's not just *my* advertising cost. Give or take a few percentage points, that's the advertising cost paid by *every* successful company I know in this business. You'd better count on it and plan on it. If you can advertise for less, good! You can put the profits aside and use them the next time you try something and it bombs. But be prepared to spend 50%.

A lawyer friend of mine told me why he thinks that the big companies survive and the little companies go under. It's not because the President of the big corporations are so smart. (I worked for a big corporation for nine months once. I couldn't believe that that many scared, stupid people could be gathered under one roof.) The secret of success for large companies, my friend said, was that they could *afford* to do inefficient, dumb things. They're rich enough to survive their mistakes.

I might add that that's not how they *got* big. It's just how they stay alive. Herman Wouk, who wrote "The Caine Mutiny," described the operation of the Navy to this effect: "A master plan, conceived by geniuses and executed by idiots." The Navy doesn't *want* their plans executed by idiots. But they have to allow for the possibility.

And you have to be financially prepared for the fact that you or someone who works for you will, from time to time, do something idiotic. Realistic planning helps—and 50% for advertising is realistic.

Just how realistic it is can be emphasized by this bit of information: There are many, very successful advertisers in the Direct Response Business who are willing, even eager, to pay advertising costs of 100%—or more—for an order!

Why? Because they know that the customer—*and what he'll buy in the future*—is worth a lot of money! Record Clubs and Book Clubs (and similar promotions) are just two examples of Direct Response advertisers who lose a *lot* of money on the initial sale—but profit very handsomely in the long run.

But I'm not suggesting, at this point, that you go in the hole on your initial sale. I don't think you should because it requires tremendous capital.

Now, let me tell you a couple of other things that should put your mind at ease about that 50% advertising cost.

First, it's just about your total "distribution" cost. It's the *force* that moves a product from you to the customer and there's no middle man in between taking his cut. You can allocate that 50%, and the product can still cost the consumer less than he would have to pay for something comparable in a retail store. That's because the retail item has to go through so many hands (and each hand has to reach into the customer's pocket and extract both costs and profits). In retail sales there are most or all of these middle-men taking their pound of flesh between the manufacture and the eventual buyer: Wholesalers, Distributors, Brokers, Jobbers, and finally, the Retail Outlet. The retail product is sold again and again an again in ever-decreasing quantities until the customer finally completes the chain—and pays all of the expenses and the profits of the purchasers who preceded him. The retailer takes the biggest chunk. He has to. To recover his costs: Advertising, display in an expensive location, "free" parking, breakage, shop-lifting, clerks, and what have you.

That's why Driect Response merchandising is the most efficient, most direct method of distribution. It gets the greatest number of products to the most people at the lowest possible cost.

So let's take a final look at mark-up. If the actual cost of a product is one dollar, here's how the various prices you might charge break down:

Sale Price	Product Cost	Advertising Cost	Gross Profit
$3.00	$1.00	$1.50	$ .50
$4.00	$1.00	$2.00	$1.00
$5.00	$1.00	$2.50	$1.50

You can see that the profit margin on a 3 to 1 mark-up is painfully slim. Because, out of that 50 cents, you're going to have to pay your own overhead costs and have something left over for yourself. If you're selling Widgets, you'd better sell them by the carload.

But, as soon as you raise the price to $4, your advertising cost goes up only by one-third, but your profit margin *doubles!* Ah-h-h, that's better.

And if you can get $5 for your product, your advertising cost goes up by two-thirds—and your profit *triples!* The net effect is that you'll make *more* money selling *half* as many Widgets at $5 than you would if you sold them at $3! Let's see how that works out:

> 1,000 Widgets at $3 each — Gross profit: $500
> 500 Widgets at $5 each — Gross profit: $750

So you can do half the work and have half the trouble—and make 50% more profit! Now the only thing that could offset your apparent windfall of profit is this consideration: Your prospect for "add-on" or "bounce-back" sales . . . additional sales to the same customer.

Will people be so pleased with your Widget that they'll want to order more for themselves and their friends? Did they buy an "Economy" Widget and do you have a "Super-Duper" Widget that they'll find irresistible when you describe it in the brochure you include in their package? Is your Widget something they'll use up and buy again next month—and every month? Will they buy lots of Attachments for your Widget to increase its usefulness? Will other Direct Response Businessmen want to rent your list of Widget buyers?

If any or a number of these things are true, and the quantity of "add-on" or "bounce-back" orders is sufficient, then 1,000 customers at a smaller profit could be more profitable in the long run than 500 customers at a higher profit.

Here's why: Because you have *little or no advertising cost* for a *re-order*; you're making a $2 profit on each $3 sale and a $4 profit on each $5 sale.

Now, let's assume that 50% of your $3 customers reorder. That's 500 reorders and you make $2 apiece. That's a total of $1000.

Now if 50% of your $5 buyers reorder, that's 250 sales times your $4 profit—or the same $1000. But the fact is that if 50% of your $3 buyers reorder, it's likely that a *smaller* percentage of your $5 purchasers will! If your $5 reorders drop to only 30%, the profit picture changes drastically. Now your profit on your $5 reorder drops to 150 sales times $4 for a total of $600.

That means that your total profit from your $3 customer (the original order plus the reorder) is $1500. Your total profit from your $5 customer is only $1350.

Why is it likely that you'll get a lower percentage of reorders on your $5 sale? Because, usually, the greater the amount of money involved, the harder it is to get the customer to part with it.

That's why you have to figure that it'll only cost you $1.50 to talk your prospect out of that first $3, but you'll need $2.50 in advertising cost to get him to part with a $5 bill.

That same kind of buyer resistance comes into play when it comes to reordering. After all, your customer only has a limited amount of money, and he has to decide who's going to get how much of it.

And now that he's gotten the original order, the honeymoon's over. All the promises, all the mystery, all the anticipation have been replaced by reality. He has the product. Whether he reorders or not depends on two things.

First—how well your product kept your promises and fulfilled his expectations. He'll probably forgive your having been a little over-enthusiastic. (He probably discounted some of your superlatives before-hand.) But he won't forgive you—and he shouldn't—if you're a liar and a cheat.

Supposedly, a few shysters have gotten away with advertising a "Sure-fire Roach Killer" and sending two blocks of wood, with instructions to place the roach on one block and crush it with the other. Or advertising a "Breast Developer" and sending a picture of a man's hand. And the story keeps cropping up about the man who got rich by placing an ad that said "Last chance to send in your dollar!" But I don't believe it.

I *did* talk to one man who said he made a lot of money selling seeds that were supposed to produce a miraculous blossom on a "money-back guarantee." He operated on the theory that many of the purchasers wouldn't get around to planting the seeds. Of those who actually went to the trouble of planting the seeds—and were rewarded for their labor with nothing at all or a few scraggly plants—most would figure that the fault was theirs or the result of bad weather. As to the rest, by the time the plant had matured—many months after they had sent for it and planted it— they would have misplaced his address. Which was just as well because he'd moved anyway. And, needless to say, without leaving a forwarding address.

To me, the interesting thing is that the "entrepreneur" who was telling of his petty triumph was obviously down-at-the heels. If he had indeed made a lot of money at his sorry little con game, he'd obviously blown it. As I listened to him, I couldn't help think of an Old World curse: "May you make a lot of money—and spend it all on doctor bills."

There was a time when the Sears catalog could unblushingly promise elixirs guaranteed to cure cancer, tuberculosis, and rheumatism. But today's consumer is pretty smart. And why not? Advertisers have spent billions educating him. He's learned at a very tender age that most of the toys that seemed so miraculous on TV are pretty shoddy in real life (and that he'll have to wait til the day after Christmas to play with them, because Mother forgot that the "batteries are not included"). He's found that he can eat a whole loaf of Wonder Bread, and he *still* won't be tall enough and strong enough to lick the big brother or sister who's been tormenting him. He's learned that he can brush his teeth after every meal with Ultra-Brite and still not be irresistible to members of the opposite sex.

All in all, with the help of Ralph Nader, he's become a little skeptical. And it's a good thing. It doesn't mean, as they say in the childhood chant, that "Cheaters never prosper." It does mean that the Cheater finds it very hard to prosper and, I hope, spends it all on doctor bills. It means that you'd better have a *unique* product that provides a *real* benefit. That doesn't mean that you shouldn't make a handsome profit. In fact, you *should* be rewarded. But remember that no man can get rich unless he enriches others. And that enrichment can and does consist of making another's life easier, or simpler, or more fulfilling.

The second reason that getting that reorder is a challenge is this: There are only four basic Human Motivations—what I call the 4 R's. They are: Reincarnation; Recognition; Romance; Reward.

Reincarnation—All of us *hope* for Immortality or Life after Death . . . and a few of us really believe in it. Most of us hedge our bets by creating works, or children, or monuments that will survive our physical being, so that at least some part of us will live "forever."

Recognition—We want the respect and admiration of others. Even if we have to inspire these reactions through fear.

Romance—Sex is the driving force, but even after the fires have been banked, most human beings have a continuing need for comfort, companionship, and tenderness.

Reward—This can take many forms: a nameplate on the door of an office; an office with a view instead of four blank walls; the services of a private secretary. But the most common, and most eagerly sought after, reward is Money. In this country at least, it's the coat-of-arms of the Aristocracy . . . the irrefutable answer to the question, "If you're so smart, why ain't you rich?"

There are only these 4 R's—and they are being assaulted by 1500 advertising impressions each day! There are billboards, newspapers, circulars, letters, radio, and they're all appealing to any or all of these Motivations, vying for the same spendable dollar. And the more they ask for—the bigger the size of the purchase—the harder it is to get. The ease of making a sale is in inverse proportion to the money it takes to complete it. Putting it another way, the farther it gets away from what the prospect will spend "on impulse"—without carefully considering the amount of money involved—the more difficult it becomes to convince a buyer to opt for your solution to his problem instead of your competitor's. Or to decide to attempt the solution of some other, apparently more urgent problem.

That is why it's harder to get someone to spend $5 instead of $3 for his original order. And that's the obstacle you have to overcome when you determine your sales price and go after that profitable reorder.

How do you set this optimum price? You don't. You let the public decide. You test in the way I've already outlined. You keep records—and you take the course they dictate.

Incidentally, there are other methods to test components in your advertising. Many newspapers have what they call "split runs." Because they're mechanically set up to print two identical pages at the same time, you can make what is called a "True A-B Split." Half of the subscribers will get the "A" copy and half will get the "B" copy. In theory, if there are two subscribers in the same block, one will get a publication with your "A" advertising copy, and the other subscriber will have a chance to react to the "B" copy. By keeping track of your results, you can decide which is the most effective.

"Regional" or "Zone" editions of magazines or newspapers are *not* meaningful in copy-testing. Even if you adjusted mathematically for the difference in the *number* of copies of the publication sold in each area, there may be geographical, ethnic, educational, or economic differences that could affect results.

In this discussion of Pricing, here are some experiences I've had that might be helpful.

In two of my businesses, I've used what I call the "3-5-7 Strategy." My basic sale is $3. But I offer the prospect a substantial saving if they order double the quantity for $5 or triple the quantity for $7. I can do this because the clerical cost is the same for all three orders (it takes the same time to slit the envelope, type up the order, and keep the accounting records, no matter what the size of the order).

The difference in packaging (materials and labor) is increased very little for a large order. (In one business, we use the same size "Jiffy bag"— a mailing package—for all three sizes of orders. In the other business, we designed a package that will accommodate a single or double order. When we get a triple order, we send one double and one single. (In both businesses, our "standardized" packaging means that we can order in larger quantities and save money.)

The differential in postage does *not* increase proportionately. Only the weight of the *product* has gone up. The packaging is the same and *one* set of instructions and literature to resell the value is all you need. (Reselling is important. They might have forgotten "why" they ordered and what your product will do for them.)

The net result is that I'm working on a somewhat slimmer profit, but I've increased the size of my "average" order—generally, to about $4.84. I've also gotten the people who might not have ordered at $5, but would spend $3, to place an order, and I've picked up some who were willing to invest $7.

The approximate percentages break down this way: 45% order the $3 package; 38% order the $5 package; and 17% order the $7 package. A thousand orders typically produces an income of $4,400 or $4.44 per order. But that's only $4.44, and I said earlier that my average order was $4.84. Where does the other 40 cents come from? I ask the buyer to "Please enclose an extra 50 cents for postage and handling." About 80% of them do. Even if they don't, we send the package anyway.

Why don't we return the order and ask for the amount due? Or at least enclose a bill? Because, in the first case, I believe that the extra handling would cost as much or more than it would produce in "collections." Besides, the delay in shipping might antagonize the customer and cause him to say "Forget the whole thing." In trying to collect 50 cents, I would risk losing the $4.44.

In the second case (enclosing a bill), I've told the customer that I've caught him trying to cheat me. Or, at the very least, I've proved that he's careless or semi-illiterate since he obviously didn't follow the instructions in the coupon. Either way, I've embarrassed him or made him angry. If that's true, he might decide to "get even" by returning the package—and I've lost a friend and a customer.

The "3-5-7 Strategy," where it's applicable, does more than allow you to offer the price that meets the lowest point of "buyer resistance" (in this instance, those who are willing to spend $3). It also enables you to capitalize on those who are willing to spend more. Furthermore, and perhaps most important, it gives people a chance to "sample" your product. If they like it, they'll buy more. In our case, our average reorder is $6.20.

The only time you can use the "3-5-7 Strategy" is when the choice lies between quantities or sizes. Not when the customer has to choose between products. Supposedly, you've offered the best solution to his problem. His only decision should be "how much" he wants to buy, not "which." If you're selling luggage, it's O.K. to offer small, medium or large. You can offer "regular" or "deluxe." But don't offer a choice between a briefcase or a two suiter or a cardboard box. It confuses the customer. And if he can't make up his mind, he *will* make up his mind—and buy nothing.

Should you ship C.O.D.? Not without a deposit that at least covers your cost. Your cost will be the regular postage, plus a special C.O.D. charge that the Post Office imposes, and the cost of return postage if the package is unclaimed. (Even after making a deposit, about 12% of your customers aren't home when the Postman comes, or don't have the money, and never get around to redeeming the package at the Post Office.) There's also a considerable amount of paper work in preparing C.O.D. packages.

All of these are *extra* costs that the customer has to pay, over and above the cost of the merchandise. For example, on a $3 order, the extra charges will be about $1. That means that if the customer sends you a dollar deposit, the Postman will still have to collect $3 (or even more, including a money order fee) for you to break even. And the customer won't be happy.

For the beginner, I recommend a line in the ad that says "Sorry—No C.O.D.'s."

Should you insure packages? I don't recommend it. The costs of paperwork and the insurance itself would be horrendous. If one of my customers says he never got his order (and a reasonable time has elapsed), I take his word for it and send him a replacement immediately. My records might show that we sent it, but that doesn't prove he received it. Recently a Post Office official publicly admitted that 9 *billion* pieces of mail are either delayed, lost, or stolen each year . . . that's about 10% of the total! The figure doesn't surprise me. Not when I see how many little pieces of paper can get lost or misplaced in an area no larger than the top of my desk. And when I think of how many hands it has to go through and the distances traveled, I'm amazed that any mail gets delivered at all.

To establish some control of those thousands of itty-bitty coupons we get every day, we've set up the following procedures. They serve three purposes: (1) Show us which ads are producing what income. (2) An accounting method so we can reasonably expect to catch anyone who might be tempted to steal a cash payment included with an order. (Yes, some people still send cash through the mail.) (3) Make sure that an order is typed and shipped.

Here's what we do: When the mail is picked up or delivered, it's sorted by "department number." That number, which appears in the coupon as part of the address, tells us which ad the customer is responding to. (I'll go into greater detail on how to "key" or "code" an ad later on.) Any mail that *doesn't* bear a department number is opened. If the "code" does appear on the coupon, (but the customer forgot to put it on the envelope) . . . or it can otherwise be identified (say, for example, that the coupon is on newsprint and the envelope or coupon bears a St. Louis address. You know that you ran an ad in the St. Louis Globe so you can reasonably assume that this order is a result of that ad) . . . and if payment is enclosed, you put the now-identified letter in the appropriate stack. If no money is enclosed, or if it's a request for information, or a complaint, it goes into a "No Money" stack.

When the sorting has been completed, a report of mail received for that day is made up. It lists the department numbers in numerical order, followed by the number of pieces of mail received for each department, as well as the *total* of the number of pieces received by *all* "departments." Remember that, at this point, none of the mail with the "department" number on the envelope has been opened.

Then, an Accounting Form is made up for each "department." It includes the department number, the total quantity of orders included as well as a space for each of the orders expected. (For example, if you're using the "3-5-7 Strategy," you'd have 7 spaces. One for a $3, another for $3.50 and so on. The last space would be for an occasional "Other"—for people who order combinations or multiples of the prices offered.) There's also a space for "extending" or totaling the amount of money that a particular order represents. (For example, in the space that says "$3," there's room to write the number 40 if that's what the mail produced, and another space to show that this comes to $120. Now there's another space

Number of Pieces _____ Dept. _____

1st Count _____ OK _____ Date_____

ORDERS

____ @ \$3.00 totaling \$_____

____ @ \$3.50 \$_____

____ @ \$5.00 \$_____

____ @ \$5.50 \$_____

____ @ \$7.00 \$_____

____ @ \$7.50 \$_____

____ Others \$_____

_____

____ Total Orders \$_____

OTHER MAIL

____ No \$ enclosed

____ Not enough \$ enclosed

____ MAIL TOTAL

CASH & CHECK SUMMARY

Cash:

____ \$10 bills \$_____

____ \$5 \$_____

____ \$1 \$_____

____ \$.50 Coin \$_____

____ \$.25 \$_____

____ \$.10 \$_____

____ \$.05 \$_____

____ \$.01 \$_____

Total \$_____

Checks:

____ \$7.50 \$_____

____ \$7.00 \$_____

____ \$5.50 \$_____

____ \$5.00 \$_____

____ \$3.50 \$_____

____ \$3.00 \$_____

Total \$_____

GRAND TOTAL \$_____

to show the total number of orders accounted for, and still another to show the total number of dollars those orders should produce.) Finally, there's a space for reporting the number of pieces of "No Money" mail and still another for "Not Enough Money."

The Accounting Form, together with the appropriate mail, is given to one of the people who opens the mail. This person re-counts the pieces. If it's correct, he puts his initials on the Form to indicate that he's received it and accepts responsibility for it. If there's a difference in the count, he adjusts it (with the approval of the supervisor who made the original count) before initialing the Form. (If the response to a particular ad is very heavy, the "department" is divided into bundles of 100 letters or less, to reduce the possibility of error and make rechecking easier.) Then the person opens the mail. (I'll continue referring to the Opener as "he," but it's usually a girl or woman.) He first verifies that the name and address on the coupon are legible. If not, he checks the address on the envelope or the check or money order, with the hope that one of them can be translated. (I'd like to have a nickel for every order we haven't been able to process because we couldn't read the name and address. And then we get a nasty letter, threatening to report us to the Post Office, the District Attorney, and the Better Business Bureau—of which we're a member—if we don't ship the order immediately . . . and we can't read the name or address on *that* letter either.)

Assuming that he does solve the puzzle when necessary, he prints the corrected address on the coupon. If the payment is by check (and the address is imprinted), and it differs from the address on the coupon, he prints the coupon address on the check (so that if the check bounces, or the account is closed, we have some idea of where to look for our delinquent purchaser.)

Another technique we use when we can't decipher a name and address is this: If the payment was by check, we write to the bank giving the account number and explaining our problem.

Next, the Opener verifies that the merchandise ordered coincides with the payment enclosed. If it's too much, even by a penny or two, he notes the overpayment on his Accounting Form. Later a Credit Memo or refund check will be issued. If it's too little, but the unpaid amount is *less* than 10% of the purchase price, he notes the underpayment on his Accounting Form. (The order will still be shipped for the reasons I outlined before.) However, if the under-payment exceeds 10%, he notes that fact on his Accounting Form in the "Not Enough Money" space. (The order will not be shipped, and the matter will be handled as I'll tell you in a few moments.) If there's no money enclosed, or if it's a request for C.O.D.

without an appropriate deposit, or a request for information, or a complaint, he leaves the contents intact and stamps the envelope with an appropriate rubber stamp. And all the while that he's been performing these tasks, he's been separating the orders into the necessary stacks—one for each category. When he's finished, he uses a numbering machine (they range in cost from $20 to $60) to imprint the identical number on a coupon, the envelope it comes in, and the check or money order that accompanies it. If an order is paid for with cash, the name and address and the amount is written on a piece of paper and numbered in the same way as the checks and money orders. (You can buy numbering machines that repeat the same number in a series of three. In other words, it'll print the number "1" three times before it goes on to "2," etc.) So now he's separated his orders by amount and numbered them in sequence. Then he puts a rubber band around each stack—one around the envelopes; another around the coupons; another around the checks, money orders, or cash, and still another around the "No Money" or "Not Enough Money" mail. (Which we'll now call "Miscellaneous Mail.") The envelopes are filed in a cardboard carton, and the coupons, the payments, and the Miscellaneous Mail all are wrapped in the Accounting Form and given to the Accounting Department.

The Accounting Department checks to see if the actual amount of money turned in "balances" with the orders reported. They do *all* of the "extensions" or final totals. The Opener does none of these figures, so he has no idea of how much money "should" be there.

If there's a shortage or overage, the coupons are rechecked to see if one or more was placed in the wrong stack. (This is usually the case when there's a descrepancy, and the error is corrected.)

If everything's O.K., the coupons are given to the typist. Since the typing demands painstaking accuracy and is deadly dull, the sequential numbering system gives the typist a safeguard against "skipping" a coupon or having one blown off her desk by a puff of wind. If, as she types the number on each label, she finds one missing, she's immediately alerted. She knows that two coupons have stuck together, or one has fallen to the floor, or she's been daydreaming. In any case, she can start her search for the cause. If she can't find the coupon, she can look up the corresponding missing number on the check or money order. The amount of the payment should provide the information she needs to replace the coupon. If payment was in cash, hopefully she can match the missing number with the piece of paper included with the checks or money orders, and the size of the order can be deduced.

Let's say that she didn't notice that a number was missing. For that possibility, she counts the number of labels she's typed and sees if it balances with the number of coupons she received. If she has fewer labels than the numbering system indicates, she can start her search.

Now let's retrace our steps for a moment. What if an Opener's Accounting Form is frequently "out of balance." Then we have to conclude that they're either unsuited to this kind of work or may be stealing. Either way, we can't afford to have them around.

How would we know if they took cash out of an envelope and then put it in the "No Money" stack? When we send out a form letter requesting payment, we enclose a return envelope that's coded with the "number" of the Opener. If we get back a few indignant letters protesting that the sender had enclosed cash—and we trace them to the same Opener—we advise him that his services are no longer required. He may be innocent, but we can't afford to take chances.

We take one additional step to save employees from temptation. No one opens mail or handles money in the Accounting Department when he's alone. At least two people must be present, and their desks must be facing each other. When they go to the restroom, or on a coffee break, or out to lunch, they go together. They do not leave the room until the Accounting Form they're working with has been completed and locked up for safekeeping.

Do I think that these procedures make it impossible to steal? No. A dedicated thief can always find a way to beat the system. But it does discourage amateurs. And I think that a more complex system for security would probably cost more than it would save.

Now, on with our story. After the orders have been typed, the labels are given to the Shipping Department. In the Shipping Department, there's one final check to make sure that no order has been missed. The labels are counted, and the total compared with the number that the sequential numbering system indicates there should be. If there's a shortage, back to the Typing Room they go. If the numbers are O.K., the labels are put on the packages. Then the packages are counted to make sure that all of the labels were indeed affixed. If a shortage develops at this point, the order can still be traced by finding out which number is missing . . . and going back to the coupon, the check, money order, or cash slip—or the envelope bearing that number.

Assuming that the errors or omissions have all been corrected, and the package has been consigned to the tender mercies of the Post Office, back to the Accounting Department. The total amount of payment received on each Accounting Form is added up. That's how much the deposit prepared for the bank should be. If the totals, taken from the

Accounting Forms and the actual deposit are "in balance," that winds up the day. If not, it's back to the adding machine and re-counting the checks, money orders, and cash until the error is discovered.

The final activity of the Accounting Department is posting the results. What they now produce is your most important record. For this purpose, you make up a sheet of paper, that can go into a binder, with these headings across the top:

"Source of Order"	the name of the publication, call letters of the radio or TV station, etc.
"Unit"	the size of the ad or the length of commercial, etc.
"Key #"	the identifying code you used.
"Day and Date Ran"	for obvious reasons.
"Cost"	the total cost of the advertising medium, including "production" charges (to have an ad set by printer, art work, a film or tape made, etc.)
"Product"	useful if you own a company selling more than one.
"Comments"	here you write anything that could have influenced results: weather, a strike, a holiday, good or bad positioning of an ad, bad reproduction, etc.

Then you write your sub-headings, so the pertinent information can be entered:

Date	Day's Orders	Cumulative Orders	Day's Receipts	Cumulative Receipts

This gives you a day-by-day picture of how your advertising is doing. It shows you what your "average" order is (divide the Cumulative Receipts by the Cumulative Orders). It gives you the pattern of results. For example, *most* morning newspapers will produce double the first three day's orders; *most* magazines will end up pulling twice as many orders as you get in the first 30 days. But they differ, and you have to know what each *particular* medium will generate in orders. The *only* way to find out is to keep records. And as you accumulate these records, you'll be able to look at what you've done in the past and be able to forecast the success or failure of a new ad in that medium. The speed of your reaction to that forecast—whether it's to expand your advertising, repeat the ad, or even cancel advertising you've already placed when that's possible—can be the difference between making or losing a lot of money.

These "Posting Sheets" can tell you "how you're doing" at a glance when you're getting started. Later, they'll tell you what you *should* do. I can't over-emphasize the importance of *keeping* and *using* them.

For practical purposes, I keep Posting Sheets "active" for 30 days after a newspaper ad has run, for 6 months after running a magazine ad. Results will still trickle in after that time. (I'm still getting about $100 worth of orders every week for ads that I stopped running over 5 years ago!) It's delicious revenue since there's no advertising cost but, statistically, it's significant.

Incidentally, I heard about one large Direct Response firm who sold out to a large corporation for several million dollars. The large corporation acquired the business because it showed such fantastic profits, particularly in the year or so preceding the acquisition. What they didn't discover til later was the reason for the sudden jump in profits. The Direct Response firm had simply stopped advertising. So they had lots of income and very little outgo!

In this business, these extra orders are called "drag." And when and if I ever retire, I expect the drag to provide me and my wife with a very fat "pension!"

Meanwhile, back at the Accounting Department . . . What happens to requests for information and complaints? *Answer* them—preferably on the day they're received. Certainly as quickly as possible. Even if a complaint's unreasonable . . . even if the merchandise couldn't possibly have been delivered in the time that's passed since you received the order . . . even if you're "sure" that the customer probably received his order a day or two after he wrote—ANSWER HIM!

Let him know, in writing and immediately, that his order—and his money—haven't disappeared . . . that all those terrible things he's heard about Direct Response companies aren't true in *your* case. It'll pay off and, someday, make you rich.

Don't do what I saw one man do, with my own eyes. I visited this character, who was running a one-man business, and watched him opening envelopes. As he slit them, he peeked inside. Some, he stacked on his desk; others he threw into the wastebasket. I asked him what he was doing. He said that he was throwing away the envelopes that didn't contain any money. He "explained" that the envelopes without money either wanted more information or were complaints. His experience, he went on to say, was that he couldn't sell the former and couldn't satisfy the latter. So he just threw them away.

Well, I'll tell you something. I could have made money out of his trash basket! Because people asking for information are *begging* to be sold. And if you take care of a complaint, you make a friend—a friend who buys.

I know another man, who's probably the best salesman I ever met. When he worked for a Real Estate firm, he *asked* to be put in charge of the "Complaint Desk." His philosophy was that once he'd solved the customer's problem—and most problems can be solved—that the customer was pleased and grateful . . . and ready to buy again from someone he trusted. It worked. He sold more property than anyone else in the firm.

A long time ago, when I was in the wholesale paper business (remember, it all started with those surplus cartons), I learned a valuable lesson. At first, if an order had gotten goofed up, I'd tell my secretary to say I was out if the customer phoned. When I finally had to face up to him, he was *mad*. Frequently, the outcome would cost me money *and* the customer.

Then I decided to try another approach. If anything had gone wrong, I'd call *him*. Preferably before he even knew about the mistake. I'd explain, apologize, and ask him what I could do to make it right. Nine times out of ten, he was so pleased at my interest that he'd tell me to forget it, or offer a settlement that was a lot less than I was prepared to give. As for the tenth man, I simply tried to settle as gracefully as possible and keep his business.

I've shown you that your BIG profit comes from reorders. Only satisfied customers reorder.

Here are some other tips to keep your costs down and improve your results. These are facts that I found out the hard way—after wasting enough money to put each of my kids through college. And I have a lot of kids.

Tip #1—Watch the weight of your package very closely.

Any advertising that you insert has to pay its own way. First, from the standpoint of what it costs to produce (including printing and amortized art and typesetting costs). Second, what does it add to your postage costs? Sometimes, you can use a lighter weight paper stock and keep the postage scale from moving up an extra notch. Then you can mail it free!

If it's at all possible, keep the total weight under a pound. Even if you have to, ship the order in two or more packages (assuming that's feasible). Because, unless you do, you can't get the savings made possible by shipping "bulk rate" (more about that later).

And as soon as you go over a pound, even if you're using ordinary Parcel Post rather than "bulk rate," the postage costs skyrocket. For example, if the package weighs less than a pound, you pay so much per ounce, no matter where you ship it in the United States. But as soon as it goes over a pound, the postage is based on the "zone" it's going to. To illustrate (at the rates in effect as this is written): you can mail a package anywhere in the United States for 60 cents or less if it weighs under 15 ounces. But if it weighs more than one pound (and less than two), it'll cost you 60 cents for local delivery and $1.05 for shipment to the furthest zone. All you can do is figure out what's best in your case—but don't forget the clerical and handling costs involved in computing the varying postage.

Avoid any product that's packed in glass. The increased costs in protective packaging—to say nothing of the weight of the glass—make it tough to market. Attractive plastic containers are cheap, lightweight, and virtually unbreakable. In my vitamin business, we use what's called "strip" packaging. Each pill is encased in an individual cellophane cell, and there are 30 cells in a "strip." This protects freshness; makes it easy to carry a day's supply in your pocket or purse. From our viewpoint, the feather-light, flat strips can be slipped into a "Jiffy Utility Bag" (one without padding) and cushioned against breakage by putting our literature on each side.

Economies like this have made it possible for us to hold our prices in this business, at the same level for the past 11 years—in spite of advertising costs that have doubled and postage costs that have soared and are continuing to rise. (Remember the penny postcard and the four-cent first-class stamp?) We do it by constantly playing the game of "What Would Happen If—." And, of course, buying pills by the millions helps.

Tip # 2—Use the lowest possible postage rate!

If you don't have enough volume (200 or more identical packages or the number of identical packages it takes to make up 50 pounds) to ship "bulk rate," use "third class." ("Bulk rate" is, at this time, roughly one-half the cost of third-class postage.)

You've heard some horror stories about the slowness of third-class mailing, and some of them are true. But first class mail can get snarled up too . . . and first class rates will kill you.

We've done test-mailings around the country, mailing three identical packages, on the same day, to the same destination. We sent one first class, another third-class, and the last as part of a bulk-rate shipment. In every case, they all either arrived at the same time or, at most, delivery was delayed by a couple of days! Although "bulk rate" enjoys the lowest cost, delivery is usually satisfactory because you're doing most of the Post Office's work for them in terms of sorting and bundling.

Sure, you'll have an occasional third class or bulk rate package go astray. When you do, replace it promptly. It's still a lot cheaper than sending everything first class.

The only exceptions I make are these: (1) Merchandise Replacements are sent first class or even air mail. If I can believe my tests, they won't arrive much sooner, but I think the psychological impact on the customer is worth the added expense. That extra postage is meant to say "I'm sorry—

and I value your business." (2) Sometimes, customers are in a dreadful hurry to get the product (for example, with Larry Voegele's book on how to beat the horses). So I've offered, in the coupon, to send the book by air if they'll pay the extra cost—and if they do, I do.

The Post Office has some bargain rates for certain kinds of merchandise. Books and records for example. Books can be sent out at a special rate. It's comparable in cost to the "bulk rate"—but without the necessity of identical package, minimum shipments, sorting, and bundling. All you have to do is write or rubber stamp the words "Book Rate" on the package. One caution: you can't enclose any advertising literature and you can't seal the package (but you can staple it).

Certain records (and I would assume cassettes, although I've never checked it) enjoy a privileged rate. All you have to do to take advantage of it is write or stamp the magic words "Educational Material" on the package.

I think it's accurate to state that no one in the Post Office will *volunteer* information on how you can save money on postage rates—or tell you that you're paying more than is necessary. But with these guidelines, persistence, and a thick skin, you can wheedle out the information you need. Always go to the Head Man; he's most likely to be well informed or know whom to ask.

The one factor that's indispensable in making lowest cost postage work is this: Fill your orders the same day they arrive. Or, at the very latest, the next day. If you're out of stock, or there's some other problem, send an explanatory card or a letter to the customer *immediately*. Don't forget: he's sent money to someone he doesn't know for something he hasn't seen—and he's nervous. He's eager to get the merchandise, or he wouldn't have ordered it in the first place. Reassure him. *Before* he complains.

Tip #3—Keep on top of the Sales Tax!

I don't know about the laws in other states, but I can tell what I *think* I know about California. (We've been "audited" three times in the past 11 years and have gotten clobbered each time. I have the uneasy feeling that every time Ronald Reagan needs a new jet or Nancy Reagan wants to redecorate the Governor's Mansion that they send a guy around from the State Board of Equalization to pick up the down payment from me.)

The only hopeful note is that the "assessment" has been for a lesser amount each time. What's discouraging is that each new auditor tells us that the instructions given by his predecessor are wrong—and *this* is the way we should keep our records. I can hardly wait til the next time. Maybe they'll discover we've overpaid. And maybe the moon really is made out of cheese.

O.K.—back to *your* problem. You'll need a resale permit number. There'll be a small fee, and you'll have to post a cash deposit (or a bond), consistent with the tax you'll owe, based on the volume of business you expect to do. There's some way that you can put the money in a Savings and Loan and earn interest, even through the principle is pledged to the State Board (ask your Accountant).

The resale permit number allows you to buy all the supplies that you resell, without paying tax. For example, you don't have to pay sales tax on your Widgets or the instruction booklet that goes with them. You do have to pay tax on the advertising literature you put in the package. There are all sorts of fascinating, trifling differentials like that, and your Accountant is, again, your best source of advice.

One sidelight: my wife uses our resale permit number to get into wholesale showrooms, who do business only with "dealers." She has to pay the tax, but she saves a lot of money. Or so she tells me.

Now, how much tax do you have to collect and remit? Well, on all sales made to customers living in the city (if there's a city sales tax) or the state where you do business, you have to pay the tax. On out-of-state sales, you do not have to either collect or pay.

Now, if you're doing a big volume and a substantial amount of your sales are out-of-state, how do you know how much is taxable—without getting buried under piles of records that you're required to keep for 3 years? One answer, of course, is to go on computer. If you're not quite ready for that (and I don't feel that I am quite yet), there's an alternative. I can't say that this method will be accepted on the next "audit," but it was the last time. Here's what we did: We selected a representative day of the week and saved *all* the envelopes that came in that day, every week. Once a month, we checked the postmarks on those envelopes and determined which were in the city and which were in the state. Then we took those totals and divided them by the total number of envelopes to get our percentage of taxable sales.

At the end of 3 months, before submitting our "quarterly returns," we averaged the percentages. Then we applied those percentage figures to our total sales for the quarter—and sent off a check. When we were audited, we had the envelopes to support our figures. (They accepted our proof; the "error" was in another area.)

Incidentally, if you are assessed, you don't have to accept their figure. You can arbitrate or appeal, and if you're in the right, I recommend that you do. We've had assessments reduced by two-thirds.

Finally, should you collect sales tax at all or simply absorb it in your price? The latter course will certainly simplify bookkeeping and require less time for making up bank deposits. It's really up to you. If you decide to collect the sales tax, *don't* put a line in your coupon that says something like "California Residents, please add 5% sales tax." That's too much of a strain on the customer. He's a buyer, not a mathematician. Prefigure it for him and ask him to enclose so many cents for sales tax.

Tip #4—Don't hold orders, waiting for checks to clear!

In the first place, it can take days or weeks—and how will you know which checks have cleared and which have not? Even more important, why should you punish all of your customers for the transgressions of a few? Trust them. Most of them will justify that trust. After all, they trusted you.

Our bank has instructions to put any check that bounces through a second time before returning it to us. When a check is returned, we write to the customer, asking him to make good and reimburse us for the fee the bank charged. Most do. From time to time, we gather up a batch of checks we have not been able to collect on, and turn them over to our attorney. For a percentage, he tries again, and we get some more of our money in. If your experience is like mine, the remaining uncollectibles are a stiff figure at the end of the year, but only a tiny fraction of your sales volume.

Tip #5—Shop around for a bank!

Banks differ widely in their policies—and those differences can add up to a lot of money for you. I've found that an independent bank, or one that's part of a small "chain," usually offers the most advantages.

Here's what you want to compare: (1) Will there be a service charge if you maintain a minimum balance—and what's the minimum? (My bank does not levy any service charges as long as my minimum balance is $200.) (2) Will they charge you for each check you deposit? (Most large banks will make a charge for each check you deposit, if you deposit a large volume of checks of small denominations. Depending on the volume, this can be anywhere from one to three cents—or even more—per check.) This seemingly insignificant amount can run into BIG money. Before I switched banks, I was being charged about $7,000 a year for this "activity"—and this was the net figure after I'd been given "credit" for the "average balance" in the account! Based on my present volume, that figure would have been multiplied again and again. My present bank makes no charge for deposits—which is exactly why it's my present bank. (3) Will they allow you to deposit checks and money orders without listing the bank numbers and itemizing the checks? (There's a procedure for doing this, attaching only an adding machine tape after the checks have been separated. A cooperative bank will show you how.) Eliminating the bank number listings and listing each check will save you hundreds of man-hours. (4) Can you bank by mail, and will the bank pay the postage? If you have a wad of checks, the postage can be two or three dollars a day. That's over $1,000 a year—and they can afford it better than you can.

After you've shopped for your best deal and weighed the other obvious considerations—like convenience of location and availability of credit for your operation—pick the one that has the most to offer. But think in terms of your future, as well as your present, needs. Incidentally, your bank can also help you file a "Certificate of Fictitious Firm Name" if one's necessary.

Tip #6—Make refunds promptly.

The only thing that I can add to that is "cheerfully." We've made some so fast that we discovered that the customer's check had "bounced" after we'd already sent him a refund. But that's more than offset by the people who are so pleased at the speed of the refund that they ordered again. (And we got our money back in most of the other cases.)

Tip #7—Read "The Reporter of Direct Mail Advertising—The Magazine of Direct Marketing"!

You can probably pick it up at your local Public Library (I recommend looking over as many back issues as they have), or you can subscribe. If you want a subscription, send $10 for 12 months to:

Direct Marketing
224 Seventh Street
Garden City, New York 11530

No, I don't make a commission (although I have to admit that the thought crossed my mind.)

But I want you to read it, because I think you'll find it chuck-full of information and help you'll want and need. Each month, it describes dozens of brand new products you might want to take on—or will trigger ideas of your own. There are great articles by some of the best Pro's in the business, examining every phase in great detail. There's a Directory, itemizing the names and address of the people who provide the services and the products you'll need. And Ideas, Ideas, and more Ideas! It's invaluable—and if you're serious about taking a crack at the Direct Response Business, you can deduct your subscription as a business expense.

Well, I've covered almost everything you need to know about Pricing and Business Practices. Plenty to get you started, keep you going, and help you *get* big and *stay* big.

None of it will guarantee success. That depends on you and what you do about your ISI! But it'll sure keep you from making the dumb mistakes I made when I was starting out.

Q. Is there any simple way to make up my shipping labels?

A. For the beginner, I recommend using "Duplistickers." There are 33 perforated labels to an 8x11 sheet—and you can buy them with the carbon interfolded, so that a single typing produces two or three copies. You can use one duplicate for a follow-up mailing and put the other on a file card. When you're ready to take the next step, you can get a photocopy machine—"copy" the sheet of 33—and produce all the labels you'll ever need for your own use or rental.

Q. How do I keep my list current?

A. By "cleaning" it. You do this, after a follow-up mailing, by removing the names that are returned to you by the Post Office as undeliverable or giving a change of address. You can also ask people who "rent" your list to return the "mixies"—those that can't be delivered.

Q. What's a good way to "key" my response?

A. We assign numbers to every publication we use. The first ad we place gives that number in the "Department," followed by the letter "A." The next one is "B" and so on. We "skip" sequential letters that look too much alike and will slow down the sorting. To illustrate, our "alphabet" is A B C D F G H J K L M O P Q R S T V X Y Z.
For radio or TV, we use a Department number, or if we're using a Post Office Box address, we add a letter. For example, "Box 345-A."

CHAPTER SIX

HOW TO WRITE SUCCESSFUL ADS

I can tell you how to write an ad in one word:

Don't.

Most people who try to write "ads" immediately adopt a stilted style. Or try to be terribly clever. Or use words that they—and the rest of us—have to look up in the dictionary. The result is a special language and form that I call "Advertise-ese." There's only one problem with it: it doesn't *communicate*. It's not *personal*. It's all skin and no flesh. And certainly no guts.

When you've found something you want to sell, here's all you have to do to create a successful ad. And I promise you that it'll work.

First, think of all the things your product will do for people. Then pick out the one, most important, *specific* thing it will do. Not just "Makes Long Life a Reality" but "Guaranteed to Make You Live to 100!" Not just "You Can Be Important!" but "How to Get a Promotion and a Raise in 5 Minutes!" Not just "You Can Be Beautiful" but "7 Ways You Can Make Him Ask for a Date!" Not just "It's Easy to Make Money" but (will you forgive me?) "The Lazy Man's Way to Riches!"

Every one of those "headlines" appealed to one or more of the 4 R's. (Remember? Reincarnation [Immortality]; Recognition; Romance; Reward.) And the strength—the drama—of your appeal to these 4 Basic Human Motivations will determine how successful you will be in getting the attention of your reader, listener, or viewer.

There's no mystery to it. (Although a lot of ad agency copy chiefs who are pulling down $50,000 a year would like you to think so.) I'm *showing* how they do it, step by step, and you can do it too! So let's continue.

Think about what you'd like the product to offer *you*. What problem *you'd* like it to solve. (You're really not that much different from anyone else.)

Write down *all* the ideas that come to you. Even if they seem silly or wild. Don't try to judge them—not yet. Just write them down. Keep a pad and pencil in your pocket or within easy reach. If you don't capture your inspiration and make it a prisoner, it'll escape and be lost forever.

I've gotten *all* of my best ideas when I was driving my car, or riding my bike, or reading a book, just falling asleep, or just waking up.

Do you notice what each of these activities had in common? Nothing. That's right, I was doing absolutely nothing about solving my problem—how to sell a particular product—and then the right idea suddenly popped up. Not out of nowhere . . . out of my Subconscious Mind.

What had I done to feed the Subconscious Mind the information it needed, so it could spit out the answer? I'd simply thought about the product. Not so much what it is, but what it *does.* My wife bought a vacuum cleaner and hired a housekeeper. But what she really *wanted* was an easy way to clean the house. Do you see the difference? People buy things or hire people, but what they're after is the *result.* If she could press a button, and through some miracle of electronics or ultrasonic sound waves, the house would be cleaned spotlessly—and the cost was within reason—she'd junk the vacuum cleaner and fire the housekeeper. (At least, I think she would. I'll have to ask her.)*

So think about what the product will *do.* Better, or cheaper, or faster than anything else you know about.

Think about all the reasons *you* would buy it. Think about all the reasons you *wouldn't* buy it. (How many of those objections can you overcome?) Write it all down. Read magazines and newspapers. Notice how articles about the problem leap right off the page and hit you in the eye. If you must, talk about the product with people who are as enthusiastic as you are. But even if you try to avoid the Wet Blankets, there's a danger. You might, literally, talk it out and release the energy you've been building up.

Because that's exactly what you've been doing: fueling the Subconscious. Warming it up. So it can produce that spark you're looking for.

When you feel you're saturated with facts and insights . . . when you've racked your brain, simply forget about the problem. The next step is to do nothing. Go on with the other things that make up your life. What could be easier? But, at that point, the problem is as good as solved. In an hour, or a day, or a week, you'll get *the* idea. The one, perfect way to express exactly what your product will do. It'll come when you're not "thinking" about it at all.

Write it down! And *keep* writing. Because the "headline" or the attention-getting idea is just the valve—and it's been blown off by the

_____
* I did ask her—and she said I was right.

pressure of the whole idea that's boiling underneath. It'll all come out now. Just keep writing. Keep writing til you run out of steam. Chances are that you won't til you're finished. But if you do, don't worry about it. Forget it again. When it's ready, the Subconscious will let you know that it's raring to go back to work.

What about all those notes you made? Don't look at them or think about them til you're finished. That's because you want to give your Subconscious Mind a chance to "edit" them—to polish up the good ones, combine some to produce a new idea, discard the ones that are unworkable or simply don't fit into your new concept.

After you're all through writing, look at your notes. There might be a phrase or two that you'll want to include. But it's not likely. You'll be amazed at how your Subconscious has sorted out your input—keeping the good stuff and rejecting the junk.

At this point, put what you've written away for a couple of days before you look at it again. Make minor corrections. Read it aloud and listen to whether it sounds like you *talking*. That's important. It should use the same words you'd ordinarily use in talking to another human being. If you've included something terribly clever or coined a great little slogan—kill it. Or it'll kill you. As soon as people become aware of your "style," you've lost them. They may be entertained. They may be amused. But they won't buy.

The next step is the hardest. Have other people read what you've written. But you're not to listen to their opinion. Not til you've had a lot more experience and know which opinions to accept and which to reject. And that takes years. At this point, the only thing you want to know is whether your ad is *clear*. Not whether they like it or dislike it—only whether they *understand* it. If they don't know what you mean, clarify it. If they have to reread a phrase before they understand it, (watch their eye movements!) change it. But don't change your approach or change a single word because they suggest one that's "more refined" or "sounds better."

After reading your ad, if they know what your product will do for them, what its advantages and disadvantages are, if they know how much it costs and where to buy it—that's all that's necessary. Why do you tell them about the disadvantages, the small weak points? So they'll *believe* you. And if you've been completely honest, they'll have to believe you. Because it's the truth. The truth, told as attractively as possible, perhaps. But still the truth.

Do you still think it is hard to write a good ad? Let me show you how easy it is.

Dear Betty,

    I love you very much.

    I want to take care of you and our kids for the rest of your lives. There'll be good times and bad. But I'll try to do my best with what I've got.

    From time to time, I'll probably exasperate or annoy you. But I promise that you'll never be bored.

    I read somewhere that the contract for marriage is the only one that doesn't have a definite term—a point at which it ends or can be renewed. It just says "Til Death does us part." Well, I want you to know that, in our case, I'm satisfied with that arrangement. But, to be perfectly honest, I sometimes wish that we weren't married—so we'd both know, every day, that we were sharing our lives because we wanted to . . . not because we had to.

                 All my love,
                 Joe

You're saying, "That's no ad. That's a love letter!" Well, *every* ad should be a love letter, a personal communication. And let's see if this one contains the basic elements.

You may not like the headline "Dear Betty"—but my wife will be crazy about it. It has her name in it, it's directed to *her.* And that's the secret of a good headline. The person reading it, the one you're trying to reach, should say, "Hey—he's talking to *me!*"

The sub-head, "I love you very much" isn't bad either. I've told her that she's a very important person, a great human being, and that I care about her.

Next, at the start of the body copy, I've made my promise—to take care of her and our kids for an unlimited time. Then I've gone on to enumerate the advantages and disadvantages of such an arrangement. (If she wasn't already so familiar with them, I'd probably have gone into greater detail and been more exact. But, after all, I made my sale some years back and am now looking for a reorder.)

The rest of the copy is simply reassuring, repeats the promise, and identifies the seller. Although there hasn't been a specific call for action, it's certainly implied. She knows what I want—which is why I married her in the first place.

As you can see, you don't have to be a literary genius to write a good ad. Not a great ad perhaps, but enough to get the job done.

Let me give you another example. Let's say that you found the following note from a friend in your mailbox:

I have a new Caddilac that I got to sell because I'm leaving for the Service next week. It cost me $8,000 and only has 732 miles on it. Rather than sell it to some thief of a car dealer or going to the trouble of advertising, I'll let you have it for $4,000.

If you don't have the cash, don't worry about it because I only owe the $4,000, and you can take over my payments (which are about $75 a month).

You know I drive careful, but I'd feel better if you'd have your mechanic check it out before you buy. In fact, if you'd like to drive it for a couple of days, I'll be glad to deliver it to you with a full tank of gas. And if you don't like the car, I'll take it back and you've had a free ride. No obligation.

One thing—it's an awful green color (but you could have it painted).

If you're interested, call me at (714) 826-1313 between 7 and 9 tonight.

Your friend,
Roger Atbury

Now, that's a good ad! It doesn't matter that your friend doesn't know how to spell "Cadillac" or that his grammar is atrocious. He's told you what he's selling, why it's cheap, how you can easily afford it, revealed its one shortcoming (correctible), offered a free trial, and told you just what to do if you want to buy.

There are still a number of reasons that you might not want to buy it—you might hate Cadillacs or not be able to afford $75 a month—but you'll have to admit that it's an almost irresistible offer. Even if you only bought it for resale.

The whole point is that a good product will *almost* sell itself—if you don't garbage it up with a lot of things that people think are "advertising."

Maybe you've noticed that I haven't said anything about how big or how long your ad should be. The answer to that is: as big or as long as it needs to be. It takes less space or time to sell a Cadillac at half-price than it does to sell a Widget. That's because the Cadillac has been pre-sold by General Motors, and all you have to sell is the bargain price and the terms—and make it believable. With your Widget, you're starting from scratch.

I never start out to write a certain size of ad. I simply write the best, most complete ad I can. I try to describe every sales feature, anticipate and overcome every objection.

Not til I'm finished and am satisfied that I've done a good selling job do I decide what media I'm going to use. A very long ad can go into a letter—or be used in newspapers or magazines if you can afford the greater risk. A short one can be used in all of those and might work even better on radio or TV. Because a small ad might be "lost" in a magazine or newspaper, but every radio or TV commercial is the equivalent of a full page. *Your* radio or TV commercial is just as important and can be just as effective as the one produced by the biggest, richest advertisers in the country.

But I won't cut my copy down to "size"—not yet. (After all, what's the point of knocking on the door if the salesman disappears when it's opened?) So, first, I'll test the ad just as I've written it. If it works, *then* I'll cut it—and test it again. If the second ad is more profitable than the first. I'll cut again and test again . . . and make my next decision, based on results. Writing advertising copy is part art, but mostly science. You can measure the effect of what you do.

What do I cut? What seem to be the lesser points, the apparent repetitions. I'll see if something can be said more economically—but *without* lousing up the ad's "conversational" quality or flow. In cutting, I use what I call the "RCA principle." First, I build the best product I know how. Then I see how many parts I can remove before it stops working.

If I cut too much, the ad won't pull as well and I'll go back to the original.

But, you say, no one will read long copy. And you're right, no one will—unless he's *interested* . . . unless it's got his *name* on it. Then he'll read every word. And that's the only guy you *want* to read your copy.

Do I turn my copy over to an artist so that I can get a "professional" layout? No. The *last* thing I want is for my copy to look like an "ad." People buy newspapers or magazines to read the news. "Ads" are a necessary but unwelcome intrusion, and the reader's experience is that many of them are overblown or untrue. So I want my copy to look like a news story (which is what it should be), matching as closely as the publication will let me, their editorial layout and typography.

So, if I want to save money, I send my copy to the newspaper or magazine, with those instructions. They'll "pub-set" it—do the job free. Or, if I'm flush, I'll take my copy to a printer or typographer and ask *him* to make it look like an article, not an ad. Ideally, the only way that the casual reader will be able to distinguish the difference between my "ad" and the editorial content will be the small "Advertisement" line the publication may put at the top. I want the printer to do everything he can to achieve that effect.

Don't use small type or a type-face that's difficult to read (again, "imitating" the editorial content is your best guide). Anything that's worth saying is worth saying aloud. And small type is associated with something you're trying to hide.

For newspapers, the "ideal layout" is usually three columns (about 5½ inches) wide and about eight or more inches deep. This size is harder for the make-up man to bury. It's likely to go on top of a larger ad. Or, if it does wind up at the bottom of the page, generally only one or two much smaller ads will be stacked on top of it. (Later, we'll go into what your position request should be.) A bottle of booze and some conversation with the make-up man are a good investment. He can tell you if there's some "shape" that's easier for him to work with, to give you the "position" you need.

I've already told you to stick with a "news" format. It's cheaper to produce and, most important, more effective. You won't win any art awards or get the admiring comments of your friends. But, with the money you'll make, you'll be able to buy your own trophies and be able to afford to move into a better neighborhood.

To emphasize my point about ads that look like ads—and are therefore suspect—here are some DON'TS.

1. Don't use "reverse" printing (white type on a black background). It may "stand out," but you've pleaded guilty to running an ad and it's also hard to read.
2. Don't use "Ben Day" backgrounds (a grey "screen" that artists seem to love). For the same reasons you shouldn't use reverse printing.
3. Don't use illustrations, unless they show the product in dramatic use—what it does, and words can't paint the picture. You're usually better off letting the prospect's imagination take over. (If I say the word "house" to you, what do you see? But if I show you a picture of a house, you may not like it—and I've stopped you cold.) What's more, the prospect may not be able to "identify" with the illustration—and you've lost him.
4. Don't get talked into a need for "white space" for esthetic effect. The publication is charging you for both paper *and* ink. Make them use the ink. It'll imprint words that'll sell for you.

Here are some other points to remember:

Restate your offer in the coupon. The customer is signing a contract—and he knows it. And you can use the space to summarize the deal and "sell" him again. Incidentally, don't make it "sound" like a contract. In conversational language—what Rudy Flesch used to call "shirt sleeve" English—tell the prospect what he's getting, what it'll do for him, and what your guarantee is. Be sure it's clear, easy to complete, and there's enough room to write the mailing information you need.

Don't use a Post Office Box as your address. It looks like you're trying to hide. Besides, giving your street address can produce an impressive number of walk-in sales. We do more than enough each year to pay the rent.

Read the large-space mail order advertising you see repeated time after time in magazines and newspapers. (That would indicate that the ads are successful.) See how well they've followed the "rules." If they've "broken" one, it may be an act of daring innovation that they've found improves results. Or the ad may be working in spite of the "mistake" . . . and the results would be improved if it was corrected. Direct Response ads have to work for a living. Every ad has to stand on its own two feet. Learn what you can from them, every chance you get.

Much "National" and a lot of "retail" advertising is wasteful. It publicizes the "name" and does very little else. It doesn't motivate people to buy. Instead, it relies on the hope that, when and if, they buy a product in that particular category, they'll remember a certain brand.

Most advertising agencies would be terrified at the thought of putting a coupon in the ad of a major advertiser. Not because, as they'd like you to believe, it would "cheapen" the product. But because it would accurately measure results—and that's the last thing they want.

In some ways, it's not the agencies' fault. They have to sell every ad twice. Once to the company that's paying the bill. And after it's been watered down, prettied up, and approved by the client's wife and 13 year old son, they have to sell what's left to the public.

A case in point is the cigarette companies. After they were "forced" off radio and TV and saved millions and millions of dollars in advertising cost, their sales went *up*. Which only goes to prove that if people really want to get cancer badly enough, they'll find a way. Or perhaps that what the cigarette companies thought was "soft-sell" was really "no sell."

We've gone pretty thoroughly into the physical production of newspaper ads (you'll see why when you read the next chapter).

Now, here are some tips for preparing your copy for other media:

Letters:

Tip #1—Send a friendly, personal letter—not an advertising circular. People like to get letters; they hate to get advertising.

Tip #2—Avoid salutations like "Dear Sir," "Gentlemen," "Fellow Fisherman," or "Dear Friend." It's a "form" letter, sure, but why rub the customer's nose in it? Don't type his name (and/or address) in either. In the first place, it's expensive; in the second place, the type probably won't match the rest of the letter and he'll feel that you're trying to put something over on him.

So, unless you can afford to go to the expense of a "computer" letter, what kind of salutation do you use? None. Just start right out with a headline—in this case, your first sentence—telling him, specifically, what problem your product will solve. If it's *his* problem, and your solution sounds good, he'll know that the letter is addressed to him.

Tip #3—Keep your sentences short and simple. Probably no more than 10 to 12 words. Keep your paragraphs short. Probably no more than five sentences.

You can send a four-page letter—and you should, if the selling job requires it—but it'll look easy to read if you follow Tips #2 and #3.

Tip #4—It'll also make the letter look easy to read—and add visual interest—if you do these things: (a) Indent some of your key paragraphs. (b) Add what appear to be hand-written notations. (c) Underline some of the important words, capitalize others. But don't overdo it. Don't, for example, put a whole sentence in capital letters. They're harder to read and seem a little pushy or "immature." (Over-selling is just as bad as under-selling. A guy has to wonder "If this deal is so good, why is he trying so hard." (d) If the letter's two or more pages long, never have a sentence end on the bottom of a page. "Carry" the reader to the next page. If possible, make that last sentence a cliff-hanger. For example, the last partial sentence at the bottom of page one might say "Forty thousand people have found that their sex" with the balance of the sentence on the next page.

Tip #5—Reproduce a *typewritten* letter, using the offset printing process. Do NOT have it typeset. Do NOT have it mimeographed. The first looks like an "ad." The second, unless it's expertly done, looks shoddy.

Tip #6—Use two colors. For the beginner, the reproduction of the typewritten material should always be in black. But the letterhead should be in a contrasting color. You can either furnish your printer with stationery if you have it, or he can give you a two-color print job. The extra expense is worth it.

Tip #7—If possible, hand-sign the letters (if the quantity's small) or have the "signature" imprinted in blue ink. (Signing with a felt-tip pen gives an impression of strength.) You can take care of Tips #6 and #7 by having the letter done in black; the letterhead and signature in blue. You can also use the blue to simulate the "hand-written" notations, but don't go wild with it.

Tip #8—Use color for added attention and a "second chance." Your letter should always be printed on white paper. But if you're enclosing a brochure or some other supporting material, use colored paper stock. A different color for each piece. Chances are your prospect will look at each enclosure before he decides to throw it away. Make each enclosure a "selling" piece. If your letter didn't "grab" him, maybe something else will.

Tip #9—Include an order form and a return envelope. (These will be at least two opportunities to add colored paper stock.) You do not have to use a postage-paid envelope. It might improve results, but that wasn't the experience of one large mailer who recently ran some tests. He reported that he got *more* orders when people had to buy their own stamps than when he enclosed a postage-paid envelope. He was surprised— and so am I.

Tip #10—Fold your letter so the printed side is out.

Tip #11—Time your mailings so they don't arrive on Monday or the day after a holiday. The mail piles up, and you have too much competition.

Tip #12—Avoid mailing during the summer months. Families go on vacation and really tear through the mail when they return.

Tip #13—Use first-class postage if you can. And if you do, rubber stamp a big "FIRST CLASS MAIL" on the envelope. The only time I "can't" use first-class postage is when the contents are so bulky that my cost would be doubled.

Tip #14—Test your mailings! I've known advertisers to put together a mailing they liked and mail out 50,000—only to have it flop. They could have found out it was a dud with a 2,000 mailing test—for 4% of the cost.

Does Direct Mail pay off? You bet it does!

Let me give two examples from my personal experience. On one item, after testing, we mailed 25,000 letters. Our cost was $3800. The mailing produced over $40,000 worth of orders! In another instance, every batch of 1,000 letters we're mailing (at a cost of $200) is bringing in $2400 worth of business! Now, these are unusually good results from a specialized mailing list. But, as of now, you know everything it took me years to find out about making Direct Mail work.

It's interesting that the newspapers grumble about "Junk Mail." But they use it themselves to sell subscriptions.

Radio:

Radio commercials can be produced in any one of three ways: (1) Live, (2) E.T.'s (electrical transcriptions or recordings), (3) Tape.

If the announcer understands some of the rudiments of selling—and realizes, as few do, that his job depends on the sponsors' success—live presentation is best. Those who ad lib, amplify, and personalize the copy can do an exceptional job. But most announcers think of themselves as entertainers and only tolerate commercials as a necessary evil. Many announcers like to demonstrate their prowess at "sight-reading" . . . their skill in being able to go on the air with a piece of copy they've never seen before. The result of these attitudes is a sing-song style of delivery, where the announcer's tongue is in gear, but his mind is in neutral. This is known as "throwing the commercial away"—along with the money that was paid for its delivery.

In the Los Angeles market, with its dozens of radio stations and hundreds of announcers, I can think readily of only two announcers whom I consider "star salesmen." The rest range from indifferent to bad.

The difficulty with radio as a medium for Direct Response advertising is the limited length of commercial time. It's difficult—and often impossible—to create desire and tell people how to order in 60 seconds. (And I wouldn't even attempt anything less.) Einstein's Theory of Relativity comes into play here: 60 seconds is a long time if you're listening and a short time if you're paying for it.

Here are some tips if you're preparing radio commercials:

Tip #1—Direct it to one person. Don't think of yourself as being in the Coliseum, addressing 100,000 people. Think of yourself as talking to a friend and saying "Hey! I've got something I want to tell you"—and then telling him. Simply and directly.

Tip #2—Don't use music to introduce your commerical or as a background. Not unless you're selling records. (And more records are sold by mail than in any other way!) But, ordinarily, music as an introduction wastes precious seconds. As background, it's distracting.

Tip #3—Allow at least 20 seconds for ordering information—the amount and where to send it. Repeat the information at least twice. If possible, three times. This repetition is annoying to the person who's not interested and vital to the person that is.

Tip #4—Don't try to use your "3-5-7 Strategy." Too many numbers confuse the listener.

Tip #5—Use a very simple address. If possible, it's best that the mail be directed to the station. They announce their call letters frequently, and if the listener missed it the first time, he has another chance to pick it up. Ask the listener to "Send $3 to Widgets in care of KDRM, Los Angeles 4," Not "Widget Company International in care of KDRM, 17242 West Hyacinth Avenue, Los Angeles 90004," Sending the mail to the station is also reassuring to the customer. He probably trusts them. He's not too sure about you.

If the radio station won't accept and forward the mail (and a few won't), it's better to use a Post Office box number than a complicated street address. If you do use a box number, be sure to identify the zone (not "90004" but "4" because it takes less time), since different Post Offices often duplicate box numbers. Try to get a box with no more than three digits and, if possible, in sequence (like "3-4-5").

Tip #6—Keep your price in even dollars. "Three dollars" is less confusing—and takes less time to say—than "two dollars and seventy-nine cents."

Tip #7—Do the commercials yourself. If you don't sound like an announcer, so much the better. The only caution is this: Don't *try* to sound like an announcer. If you stumble and stammer a bit, that's great. (Unless you're selling a course in diction.) It only adds to your believability. And people buy things from people they trust. It'll take a little practice, but you're better off ad-libbing from a "fact sheet" instead of a script. That's because you're not accustomed to reading material and making it sound as though it's coming off the top of your head. And a "spontaneous" presentation is the best kind.

TV:

It's too bad, but there are very few stations that will allow you to do "live" commercials any more. Live commercials are more effective because they have a greater sense of immediacy and can be varied from one commercial to the next. They're especially good if a product is being demonstrated, because the customer can see whether it really works or not. They're hoping it won't, but they're impressed when it does.

However, most commercials are on tape, and a few are on film.

Here are some tips:

Tip #1—Re-read all the tips on producing radio commercials. Almost all of them apply to TV.

Tip #2—Don't clutter your commercial up with special effects. The technicians love to show off their electronic wizardry, but it just reminds the audience that what they're watching is staged. The impression you want to give is that you're in his living room and talking only to him.

Tip #3—Don't read your commercial. If you must, memorize it. If you can, ad lib it. But don't ever read it. They call those cue cards that are held alongside or above the camera "idiot sheets." Don't be an idiot and use them. In the first place, you'll sound like you're reading. In the second place, you'll lose direct eye contact with the viewer. And who'll buy from someone who won't look him in the eye?

Tip #4—Don't use a "super" (printing that's imposed on a picture) unless it's absolutely necessary. It divides the prospect's attention. If you do use them, be sure that the talk matches the sign word-for-word. Otherwise, the prospect gets confused or suspicious because he's hearing one thing and seeing something else. What you're buying—the impact of sight *and* sound—is lost.

Tip #5—Ask the cameraman or director for a "medium" shot. The picture of you (if you're doing the selling) should be from slightly above the waist. That matches the way people would see you if you were visiting them in their home—and that's exactly what you're doing. A "close-up" makes you look pushy. A "long shot" give the impression you're afraid to come close. You may be talking in a conversational tone (and you should) but his eyes will tell him that you've raised your voice in order to be heard. It's just plain not intimate—and TV is an intimate medium.

Tip #6—10,000—Keep it simple. Keep it simple, etc.

Magazines:

All magazines are produced by letterpress or offset printing. In either case, your preparation is exactly the same. Most magazines will pub-set your ad (Remember—do the typography free?), but I prefer to send them a finished ad for reproduction. It saves time and the chance of error. If it's "offset" (a photographic process) that's all they need. If it's letterpress (which means that a "plate" must be made), I ask them to make the plate and charge me for it. It'll probably cost me less and will certainly save me the trouble and expense of carefully packaging a plate.

Don't ever send the magazine your "original" layout. The printer can "pull reproduction glossies" or use a photographic process to make as many "velox prints" as you'll need. In the latter case, save the negative so you can order more.

All magazine (and most newspaper) space is sold by the "line." There are 14 lines to the inch—and one inch is usually the minimum.

How big should your magazine ad be? As big as it needs to be. You can use a *slightly* smaller type-size in magazines because the paper stock they generally use reproduces more sharply than newsprint does. But don't use type so small that it discourages the reader. I've seen ads with type so small that it looked like the typographer's hobby was inscribing Bible verses on the head of a pin. I've "seen" them—but I haven't read them.

I usually run fairly large space in magazines. Two-thirds of a page or full pages. First, because I have a lot to say. Second, I think that, psychologically, it makes the offer look important and the company solvent (at least we had enough money to pay for a big ad).

I suggest that when you're ready to try magazine advertising, that you wait until you can afford to buy big space. More advertisers go broke by not spending enough to do the job than as a result of spending too much. Personally, I'd rather be chewed up by lions than tickled to death by ants.

In addition, big space gives you the muscle you need to get the positioning that can mean the difference between failure and success. (More about that in the next chapter.)

Here's one tip that can save you a lot of money:

The best months for Direct Response results are generally January, February, March, April, and May. June is shaky and July, August, and September can be disastrous. In October and November, business bounces back, and December is iffy.

So time your ads for those prime months, unless you have a

seasonal product. For Christmas items, October is the month to advertise in magazines. And November issues are good if they're "on-sale" before the 15th of the month.

Speaking of Christmas items, my experience in newspapers is to advertise after Halloween and before November 15th. Period.

The thing to be careful of is that the months you're buying in are those that the magazine goes *on sale*. The "issue" on the cover of the magaine may be an entirely different matter.

It may be the "January issue," but if it goes on sale (copies are mailed or put on newsstands) about December 15th, you could be in a lot of trouble.

So I buy the February issues that are on sale *after* January 1. Some small magazines post-date their issues by several months. For example, the "July issue" hits the newsstands in April. I presume that this is to give their product a longer life before it's out-dated.

So now you know how to write an ad and the basics of preparing it for newspapers, direct mail, radio, TV, and magazines.

Now, how do you make your best buys—and avoid the pitfalls—in buying these media? That's what you'll find out in Chapter VII.

CHAPTER SEVEN

HOW TO GET THE BEST BUYS IN TIME AND SPACE

Some time back, I said that I would tell you everything I know about the Direct Response Business. And I've tried to keep my promise. But now I'm getting into an area where I can't tell you "everything." Not because telling the truth would hurt me. But because it might embarrass and harm people I do business with and who have relied upon my discretion.

The "secret" I can't reveal is the names of the newspapers, magazines, radio, and television stations that will sell your product for you on a "commission" basis—the people you pay only for the orders they deliver. With this kind of arrangement, of course, you can't lose. Every order represents a small but sure profit.

You'd be surprised at some of the Big Name Media who are willing to be a partner in your business—provided (and this is important) they are convinced that you are reliable and honest.

This kind of a deal is called a "P.I." The letters stand for "Per Inquiry," because you pay the media a percentage of the sale price for each "inquiry" or order they generate.

Although many of them might go along with a lesser percentage, I pay them 50%. In the first place, I've "budgeted" for this expenditure. In the second place, I want them to make money. Because, if it's profitable to them, they'll give my advertising the greatest possible exposure and increase my volume of sales . . . without increasing my overhead. And don't forget that although my profit on the original order is limited, the profit margin skyrockets on the reorders I'll get— because I have virtually no advertising expense!

In "P.I." deals, the mail is generally directed to the media. After they've verified the number of orders, they forward it to you.

In addition to the "P.I." deals that can be negotiated, there are two other ways to buy space or time that have almost the same effect.

The first relates to magazines and is called "H.I.N." or "Help If Necessary." This means that you agree to pay for the ad, but if the results aren't profitable, the publication will run the ad again without charge. And will run it as many times as they have to in order for you to at least break even.

Since the orders are being directed to you, how do they know how many orders you received—and whether you need "help"? They don't. They have to trust you. And, of course, they make this deal only with people they trust. In a sense, it's self-policing. Obviously, you will want to continue buying a magazine that produces profitable results. And it might be a little awkward if you asked for "help"—and then came back in a few months and said that you'd like to run in the same magazine again. Why would you want to do that if the first time was unprofitable? Naturally, the *best* reason for playing it straight is because that's the most rewarding business practice in the long run.

The second way to reduce your risk, and this applies to radio and TV stations, is the "Guaranteed" deal. Some of the stations that won't "P.I." will go along with this one: You buy the time, and they run your "spots" (that's what broadcast commercials are called). However, if you don't get a prearranged number of orders, they'll keep running your commercials until that number is reached. Again, it doesn't pay for you to be greedy—or they won't make the same arrangement a second time.

Why are some of the media willing to be "commission salesmen"? Because they've made a commitment and are working against a deadline.

A publisher, for example, has to decide long in advance how many pages he's going to print. He allocates a certain amount of space to editorial and the balance to the advertising he hopes he can sell. If, as the deadline approaches, he has unsold space, he can do one of three things: (1) Fill the unsold advertising space with editorial—which means he has not only lost the revenue he hoped for, but he'll have to pay someone to write it. (2) He can run "Public Service" ads—free. "Smokey the Bear" is nice, but what's really going up in smoke is advertising revenue. (3) He can make a "P.I." or "H.I.N." deal with some Direct Response advertiser.

Why a Direct Response advertiser? Because: (a) He's the only kind of advertiser who can make an immediate decision without checking his "budget" or submitting the proposal to a committee (and don't forget, time is running out). (b) He's the only kind of advertiser who keeps exact records of his results and is willing to pay accordingly.

So the publisher gambles. He knows that he'll at least get some income—and if a deal is "hot," he may wind up making more money than if he had sold the space outright!

Radio and TV stations are under pressure, not day by day like a newspaper, not weekly or monthly like a magazine . . . but minute by minute. The 60 seconds that just passed is gone forever. Unlike the publisher, who can cut his product cost by reducing the number of pages he prints, the broadcaster has a fixed commitment to stay on the air so many hours a day—and his overhead grinds on. That's why the majority of broadcasters will take on at least a few "P.I." or "Guaranteed" accounts—and why some subsist on very little else. In fact, I've heard that there's a big station in Texas that won't take anything *except* "P.I.'s." They found that, if they picked the cream of the crop of Direct Response offers, they could sometimes get more income from each "spot" than if they sold it to a "national" account or a retailer! And they eliminated the need for (and expense of) salesmen and were always "sold out." Not a commercial minute was wasted!

You can use these "commission" arrangements to get started if you have little or even no capital. However, I have to be honest and say that I don't use these methods to "test" a new product or a new ad for an established product. Instead, I test in media that I've used for a long time and have extensive records on, so that I can judge the results objectively. "P.I.", "H.I.N." and "Guaranteed" deals are in a sense "artificial" and don't allow me to make direct comparisons.

After I've tested, and I know that a product is "hot," I'll make a publisher or broadcaster my partner—but not til then. Because, if it's a "proven" product, and the results are poor, my "partner" knows that it's the weakness of his medium—and won't find the fulfillment of his obligations as painful. If it's a run-away success, we're both happy. In either case, he'll call me again when he's in trouble.

There's one other circumstance in which I use these no-risk techniques. That's when someone is trying to sell me on advertising in his medium—and I have serious reservations. Perhaps I feel that the cost is too high for the number of readers, listeners, or viewers. Or I doubt that the audience composition (by sex, age, or interest) is suitable. If he thinks it is, I ask him to prove it—by taking a share of the profits. I *know* my offer "works." The only thing that's in question is whether his medium will or won't. If he's willing to gamble, fine. If not, I probably haven't missed much. You can dribble away a lot of money, a few dollars at a time. No medium is "cheap" if it doesn't produce results. No medium is "expensive" if you have a profit after paying the bill.

Now, how do you go about buying media when you're prepared to risk cold cash?

First, you take advantage of all the "discounts" that exist. Here are some tips:

Tip #1—You buy at "wholesale."

That means that you pay a rate that is far lower than the one that's printed on the rate card . . . the price that the medium quotes (and is being paid by the majority of "uneducated" advertisers).

Rate cards, particularly in the case of low-circulation magazines, quote the "asking" price. If you know what you're doing, you can pay a lot less. I'd say that in many cases I pay 20 to 50% less than the "list price." In a few instances, my under-the-table discount is even more.

I'm not trying to imply that I'm getting any bargain. The price I'm paying is what the medium is really worth. At the price I'm paying, my ads will pay off. If I had to pay any more—anywhere near the "asking price"—the results would be marginal . . . and I *could* lose my shirt.

I recently asked one of the magazine sales representatives who, among his clients, paid the rate card prices. He replied "Almost everybody. All of the 'national' advertisers and all of the 'one-shot' mail order advertisers."

"But," I said, "you know that a mail order advertiser can't pay those prices and make a profit."

"I know," he said, "but if a man doesn't *ask* me for a lower price, am I going to volunteer it? Besides, most of the little guys don't know what they're doing anyway—and wouldn't make out if they paid half of what you're paying. I'm doing them a favor, showing them that they ought to get out of the business.

"Once in awhile," he went on, "some little guy pays me top dollar and almost breaks even or maybe makes a little. Him, I'll help. I won't cut the price, because I'd be admitting I got to him the first time. But since I know that he's got the makings of a steady advertiser, I'll give him some 'free' space every so often. That way he thinks I'm a hero, and he ends up paying what he should have been paying right along."

Incidentally, this sales representative is a very nice guy, and I've never caught him in a direct lie. Some omissions perhaps, but never a direct lie. Which is more than I can say for a few of the "reps."

Now, the key words in that whole speech are "steady advertiser." And you can add to that, the advertisers who buy big units of space—full pages—and lots of them. Because those are the guys, naturally, who get the deals.

Tip #2—If there's no discount off the rate card, here's what to ask about: "Remnants." So many large magazines and newspaper supplements are putting out "regional" editions these days that there's an advantageous situation for the Direct Response advertiser. A large "national" advertiser buys one or more of these "regions" because he only has distribution in those areas. He pays a premium because he's only buying a selected part of the circulation. But you can pick up the unsold balance of the circulation at a substantial savings. However, these "remnants" are usually available only in space units of one-half page, three-fifths of a page, or full pages in the case of newspaper supplements like Parade and Family Weekly—or two-thirds of a page or full pages in the slick, big circulation magazines. And even with the "remnant" discount, the amount you have to shell out can make you pucker a bit.

Tip #3—Buy through a Bulk Buyer.

There are a handful of people in this business who contract with magazines to buy a large number of pages throughout the year. There are others who trade something the magazine wants in the way of goods or services for their value in advertising pages. Their gimmick, of course, is that they acquired what they traded or bartered for a lot less. In effect, these Bulk Buyers guarantee that the magazine will have a certain number of ad pages in every issue. In return, the magazine gives them a very attractive price per page.

The Bulk Buyer fulfills his contract by running advertising for those products he owns or has a proprietary interest in—and sells off the rest for what he can get. What he can get may vary from a 10% discount to a 40% discount. Or whatever. The only rule is that he can't sell to advertisers who are already using the magazine.

Tip #4—If you handle your own advertising, form an advertising agency.

This is really a very complicated procedure. You will need a business license and some stationery. On second thought, you might not need the business license. As a result of this tremendous investment, you might get a 15% discount on any advertising you buy! (The only exception is your local newspaper. They will probably give you a much greater discount, but it will be in the form of the "retail rate" as opposed to the "national" or "general" rate they charge the out-of-town advertisers.)

Your local radio station will give you a "retail" rate *plus* the advertising agency discount. True, some of the stuffier, old-line Media may not "recognize" you as a bona fide advertising agency (there are certain criteria for financial stability and the number of accounts you service), but most of the smaller ones and many of the medium size ones will. Particularly if it's clear that that's the only way they're going to get your business.

Tip #5—There are still other ways to save money buying advertising. That's to make a deal with someone who's contracted to buy, say,12 pages at a 20% discount (right off the rate card). But they've bitten off more than they can chew. So they'll sell you some of that space for less than you'd have to pay otherwise.

Instead of making a "P.I." deal with a broadcaster or publication directly, you can work through a Broker. If you have a good product, with a proven track record, there are two or three people (generally, Bulk Buyers) who will act as a middle man.

However, they will want the mail directed to them, will open the orders, and keep *all* of the money til they've covered *their* costs. Which means that until income reaches that point (and it may never come) you don't get a dime. From that time forward, you only get a prearranged part of the income.

Even if you could live with the financial aspects of the deal, there's another (and in my mind, more serious) drawback. There's an unavoidable slowdown in the time it takes for the mail to go to them and then be forwarded to you. This is aggravated by the fact that they'll take anywhere from a week to a month to get around to processing it. So the longer the deal runs, the greater the percentage of complaint letters. The Brokers couldn't care less. But you should.

If you've gotten the impression that buying advertising is, for the novice, like walking through Central Park at midnight without a gun— you're right. But at least I've given you a water pistol. Which is more than I had when I started. And believe me, I got mugged more than once.

But really, I've told you more than you need to know at this stage of your career. Because you should test your ads right in your own home town before you try to slug it out in the Big Leagues.

When you're ready to make the move up, contact some—or all—of the people whose names I'll give you later.

However, for the moment, let's assume that you're going to start modestly, right in your own backyard. (I still do, on every project.) Here some things you should know about it.

Newspapers:

I prefer testing in newspapers. Production's easy and cheap (I've already gone into that). You can generally assess your results in two or three days (I covered that, too). And here are some tips:

Tip #1—Don't run your ad in the Mail Order Section, if the paper has one.

Readership is poor and, generally, your ad has to conform to a restricted size and layout. The only person I can imagine poring over the Mail Order Section is someone *hoping* they'll find something—anything—to buy. Or maybe someone who's in the business and is curious about what his competitors are doing. If you think those ads "must work," because there are so many of them, save a few issues. You'll see how few are *repeated*. The only ones I see, week in and week out, are the guys who invite you to "write for free information" and then try to sell you a correspondence course for several hundred dollars. And I'll bet that even this handful of successful advertisers would do better if they took this next tip.

Tip #2—Put your ad in the Main News Section.

If there are two or more sections of Main News, try to get it in the first section. You might think that an ad directed primarily to women should be in the Women's Section or Society Section. Or if you're looking for male customers that you'll find them in the Sports or Financial Section. You're wrong. Placement in the Main News Section gives you your best exposure to either or both sexes. The only exception to this rule that I've found in 11 years is Larry Voegele's book on Professional Handicapping. These ads do best on the "Race Entries page." Presumably, the racing fan doesn't read anything else.

Most newspapers won't give you any static about getting into a particular section. But here's where you start running into trouble. Because here's the rest of what you should have, in terms of "position," for your ad to succeed.

It should be on the right-hand page. It should be "above the fold" (the "fold" is the horizontal middle of the paper if it's a standard-sized newspaper). And, if possible, it should be on the "outside edge" or, as it's sometimes called, the "thumbnail position." You can see how it got its name if you'll notice where your hands are when you hold a newspaper.

Now, to the degree that the position of your ad follows this formula, it will increase your chance of success. To the degree it varies from this position, your likelihood of failure is multiplied.

Newspaper salesmen can show you all kinds of surveys to "prove" that it doesn't make any difference where your ad appears. I can only say that I've spent millions of dollars of my own money, making my own survey—and my records show it makes a lot of difference!

If it doesn't make any difference, why don't they put their front-page news in the middle of the paper and the Classified Section on the front page? Believe me—the closer you get to that front page, the more likely it is that people will read the "news" of your product.

Now, how do you try to insure that your ad will appear where you know it'll do the most good? Well, you could weigh the newspaper—and whichever day of the week the newspaper is consistently the lightest (has the least number of pages) . . . that's the day you want to schedule your ad for. Because that's the day that the newspaper will doubly welcome your business. The paper's lighter because it has fewer ads. Therefore it'll be easier for the makeup man to give you the position you request—and you have less competition for the customer's dollar.

I avoid the hernia-inducing Sunday papers. Unless I put my ad in the Comics—yes, the Comics, or in the TV Magazine. (When I buy the TV Magazine, I request a right-hand page towards the back. That way, my ad hasn't been "lost" after they've looked at the Sunday or Monday program listings—and I'll pick up some people who'll thumb through to see what's coming up.) And I've had some success with very large ads on the front page of the Classified Section.

Tip #3—Sign a contract—the smallest (the one that involves the least obligation) that's available.

That's because newspapers have an "open rate"—which is their highest rate—and a series of "contract rates" which mean that the more advertising you run, the less it costs you per "line" or inch.

If you buy at the "open rate," you'll pay the same high price every time you run. (Although some newspapers will permit you to try one ad at the "open rate" and then back-date a contract when you run a second.)

The reason you want the smallest contract is because, if you exceed it, you'll get a rebate at the end of the year on all the advertising you've bought—based on the contract level you reach. On the other hand, if you shot too high, you'll be "short-rated." If you are "short-rated," you'll be billed for the difference per line for the contract you signed and the rate you actually earned. This can be a tidy sum. For your second year, you'll have a better idea of how much space you expect to use and can sign a contract for that amount.

Don't sign a contract that guarantees you'll run every week. Instead, sign an annual "bulk space" contract (usually 500 to 1,000 "lines"—or 36 to 72 inches).

Tip #4—Don't run just before or during Holiday weekends, or on any Holiday that falls in the middle of the week, or just before Thanksgiving or Christmas.

Tip #5—Don't buy "throw-aways" or "free circulation" newspapers. They don't work.

Tip #6—Be wary of newspapers with less than 100,000 circulation. Their "C.P.M." (cost per thousand) subscribers is ordinarily too high. But I know a few that pay out handsomely.

Tip #7—Don't let anyone kid you that repetition improves results. In the Direct Response Business each ad has to stand on its own two feet. If your first ad lays down and dies, a second ad will only do worse.

In fact, if your first ad's results are excellent, expect the returns to decline from then on. When you run an unprofitable ad or two after a series of winners, get out of the newspaper for awhile. Let the deal rest for at least a month or two—and then try it again. Sometimes a change of headline will perk it up.

The greatest thing about using newspapers—and radio and TV—in your town is that you can buy them for far less than I or any other out-of-town advertiser can. No matter how much money we spend, *you* have the advantage of a much lower cost. That's because these media, as I told you before, have a "national" or "general" rate for me, and a "local" or "retail" rate for you. Despite all the money I spend, and the advertising agency discount I'm allowed to take, you still have me beat. An ad that might be barely profitable for me could be a bonanza for you—due to your lower advertising cost. Do you remember me telling you that this is one business in which you can successfully compete with the Big Guys . . . where being "small" is actually an advantage?

So, if you're ready, contact the newspaper's Retail Sales Department and talk to the salesman. And when you're to buy advertising in other town's newspapers, your salesman can tell you how to go about that.

Radio:

Without further ado . . .

Tip #1—Stations that feature Talk Shows, All-News formats, and Country and Western music are usually effective, and in about that order. Stations that program Contemporary music, Middle-of-the-Road music, and Classical music usually won't work—unless your product is targeted towards that special audience, and even then they're doubtful.

The reason is that people *listen* to Talk Shows and News—that's why they tuned in, and they hang on to every word . . . even your commercial. They have what's called a "foreground" sound. I'm not sure why Country and Western formats are productive, but they sometimes are. Maybe because the fans have a loyalty to the announcers; have more confidence in them than those "fancy-talking dudes."

Contemporary, Middle-of-the-Road (those "good old songs"), and Classical music stations usually aren't productive because they provide a "background" sound. There are some exceptions, but you can blow a lot of money finding out which ones they are. Unless you can get a "P.I." or buy on a "Guaranteed" basis.

If you're thinking about buying radio time, *listen* to the station. If you hear a lot of spots in which the "tag" of the commercial suggests calling a phone number, or there are some Direct Response advertisers, it might be worth a try. If these advertisers continue week after week, they know something. Because the phone calls must produce "leads" for salesmen, and the orders must be coming in to the Direct Response companies—or they wouldn't continue to advertise.

It doesn't matter whether you "like" the station or not. The only thing that counts is how productive it is.

If you do decide to buy some time, place your schedule where other advertisers who measure response are.

Tip #2—Run *enough* spots.

Unlike newspapers or magazines (where repetition often depreciates results), broadcast response builds. Maybe they turned in on the middle of your commercial, or maybe they missed the address. They need another chance to get it all. Or maybe they just need convincing. Reading is active—they have to decide to do it. Listening is passive—they can just sit and let it happen.

But a one-week test is all you need to decide whether to continue or not. If I have enough orders at the end of the first week so that the total gross income is at least enough to pay for the advertising, I'll renew my contract. If it's a little less, I'll either gamble and renew—or take a week's hiatus to check it more carefully. If it's a lot less, I'll cancel for good. If I do continue, I'll do so for one week at a time—and stay on top of the results. But don't forget, as you go ahead, that the weekly results have to increase sharply (because most of the mail is coming from the previous week or weeks). If they level off, cancel.

Tip #3—If the station puts more than one commercial in a "break," make sure that yours is the first. That'll give your customer a chance to write down the address while the next commercial is on and before the program resumes.

Tip #4—Just because you go to bed early, don't forget that a lot of people don't. If you live in a metropolitan community, there's a whole army of people who don't get off work til midnight—and there are a lot of insomniacs, too. Some of your most effective commercial time is after midnight—and your costs are rock-bottom. You'll be surprised at the results if there's a personable, low-key host on the show. "Night people" are lonely, and they show their loyalty to the friendly host by buying what he sells.

Tip #5—If the station has some good "salesmen announcers," you'd be wise to submit a "fact sheet" instead of a cut-and-dried commercial. They'll ad-lib, covering your main sales points, and you'll probably end up with a "pitch" that's considerably longer than the 60 seconds you paid for. And the longer they talk, the more they sell.

If there are several "personalities" on the station, it doesn't hurt to set up a little competition. Make your mailing address "Send $3 to Widgets, care of Michael Silvertongue, KDRM, Los Angeles 4." I've never seen an announcer yet who didn't think he was the best of the lot—and was insecure enough to have to prove it.

Tip #6—Don't run a commercial directed at men during what the stations call the "traffic hours." True—there are a lot of them listening, but it's hard to write down an address when you have at least one hand on the steering wheel.

Tip #7—You, too, can be an advertising agency and save 15%!

To get started, just call the radio station and ask for the Local Sales Department—and talk to the salesman.

TV:

I spent 12 years in TV, running an advertising agency and working as one of those salesmen-announcers (do I hear someone saying "pitch-men"?) I made a lot of money—and blew it all, plus another $50,000 trying to produce my own TV show.

That debt was the best thing that ever happened to me. It made me desperate enough to try anything—and I found Dyna/Psyc.

I stopped working the 18-hour days, 7 days a week . . . a schedule that had literally paralyzed me three times. (The diagnosis was "exhaustion and nervous tension." The last time I was in the hospital, the doctor conducted a bunch of tests—including the one where they stick a tube in your scrotum and thread it through the arteries leading to your heart. After 10 days of delightful experiences like that, the doctor came to my bedside. "Well," he smiled, "I can tell you a lot of things that *aren't* wrong with you." When I got the bill for $2,000, I knew why he was smiling.)

With Dyna/Psyc, I did a lot less work—and made a lot more money. (The other day a friend of mine said, "You're the only guy I know who retired first—and *then* got rich!")

The only reason I've told you all this is partly self-indulgence, but mostly to establish my credentials as knowing something about TV.

Here are some of the things I know about buying TV time:

Tip #1 — Buy "fringe" time—daytime until about 6 o'clock at night; or after 11 p.m. You're right—you don't get the big audiences that the prime-time shows deliver. But you don't pay nearly as much per person for the ones you do reach. And many stations will permit 90-second or even 2-minute spots in these "fringe" periods. And you need all the time you can get. You have to tell before you can sell.

Tip #2—Get your commercial *within* the program. Not at a "station break." Not just after opening credits (the name of the show). Not just before closing credits (the names of the technicians).

Tip #3—If there are two or more commercials in a break, fight to be first.

Tip #4—Before you buy time on a station, watch the programs. Buy time in those where you see other "lead" deals and Direct Response advertisers. There may be a waiting list. Good—wait.

Tip #5—Don't buy spots in half-hour programs unless you can nail down Tips #2 and #3. Old movies are your best bet. I love 'em myself, but the people who watch films from England or dubbed foreign films either don't buy enough or there aren't enough of them. Adventure, cowboy, and tearjerker films work best. Comedies are so-so. Action programs, like Roller Games and wrestling can be a gold mine. Talk Shows, particularly if they involve controversy, can be very productive.

Tip #6—Remember I said that, on radio, the All-News format can work. But don't buy News programs on TV. In the first place, they're terribly expensive—and that's all the places you need.

Tip #7—Like radio, and in contrast to publications, your commercial will benefit from repetition. But, for the purposes of testing, you don't need as many spots because you have both the customer's eyes and ears to absorb the ordering information. If there's a late movie five nights a week, you might try one spot in each of three nights. Since they know what movies they're going to show, pick the ones that fit the criteria I gave you in Tip #5. And if they're having a Foreign Film Festival, watch and enjoy it—but don't buy any commercials in it. And don't sign a 4-week or a 13-week contract until you've completed your test.

Tip #8—One kind of Late Night program to avoid is the one where *all* of the advertisers are local merchants. These are usually the result of the station selling a block of time to a promoter. He, in turn, high-pressures and sweet-talks the barber, the pool hall, and the pizza parlor into advertising on TV. The price is ridiculously low—and not worth it.

Tip #9—Remember that advertising agencies get a 15% discount and a few of them will earn you more than they cost. Darned few/
When you're ready to try TV, call the station and ask for the Local Sales representative.

Magazines:

I've already alerted you to the fact there are lots of "inside deals" in this area. A few magazines stick by the rate card, but you could put them all in one stack and get over them without jumping. To clarify, I don't mean that they play footsie with the "national" advertisers (although more and more of them are buying "bartered" space). But magazines *normally* give a discount to mail-order advertisers. And some, as I've indicated go a lot further.

Here's a rule of thumb: If, based on the rate for a *full page*, the cost is about $2 per thousand of circulation, you're on pretty safe ground. I've paid a little more for a highly specialized audience I wanted to reach—and I frequently pay half that much—or less. To put that $2 figure in mathematical terms: a magazine with a *paid, audited* circulation of 1,000,000 should have a page rate of less than $2,000. Less 15% for the advertising agency. If you're, in fact, the advertising agency, your net cost should be $1,700. To the degree that you pay more than that $2 per thousand figure, you're increasing your risk. To the degree that you pay less, you increase your chance to make a profit. And profit is the name of the game.

What percentage of the readers will respond to an offer? I don't know—and I don't care. All I watch is expense (what the advertising cost) and income (how many dollars it produced). For example, if an ad cost me $2,000 (the fictional rate for a magazine with a circulation of 1,000,000), I'd want to get at least $4,000 worth of orders. Or, to put it another way, my income should be double my cost. And if you're going to grade results, that would be somewhere between "good" and "excellent."

If I've budgeted correctly, that dollar income should give me a fair profit. And I can drop down some, without losing any money. But every dollar that comes in over the $4,000 figure is half-profit! Because, in a sense, I've already paid for the advertising—and the rest is free!

However, if you insist on reducing this to percentages, it might be instructive. You'll see how few people you can reasonably expect to respond. (And maybe I'll never have to listen again to the starry-eyed people who say, "The circulation of the Times is over a million—and if only two or three per cent send in orders! . . .")

So let's proceed with our conversion to percentages: Let's say that you have a $5 offer. You need 800 orders to produce that $4,000 income. And 800 is eight-hundredths of one per cent! If it's a $10 offer, you'd need 400 orders, or four-hundredths of one per cent. Or if it's a $3 offer, you'd need 1,333 orders, or thirteen-hundredths of one per cent.

Now, these percentage figures are not what you can "expect" to get—they're what you can *hope* to get—IF the ad is successful.

Why is it so low if you're selling something that "everyone" should want? Because: (1) Some of the people who get the magazine won't read it. (2) Some of them will read only part of it—and your ad may not be in that section. (3) If they do read that section, some will not "see" your ad. (4) Out of those who see it, many will not read it. (5) Out of those who read it, some will not believe it. (6) Of those who do believe it—and mean to act on it—some will forget or never follow through.

Pretty discouraging, isn't it? Not at all—if you're prepared for it and set your sights accordingly. In other words, if you're not like those people who say, "The circulation of the Times is over a million—and if only . . ."

So what percentage of people will respond? Enough—if you're lucky.

Buying magazine advertising requires a lot bigger nest egg than any other media. Because, if you haven't established a credit rating with them (and they're tough), you have to pay in advance. That means 60 to 90 days *before* your ad appears, if it's a monthly publication. If they have extended you credit, you have to pay within 10 days after the magazine comes out to get a "cash discount" of 2%—and no later than 30 days if they're ever going to extend credit again.

Remember that I told you the "average" monthly magazine will, in 6 months, double the number of orders it pulls in the first 30 days? Well, that's O.K. for projecting income and making a decision as to whether to buy the magazine again. But it also means that you're going to wait quite awhile to get your advertising money back—and pay for the product, packaging, postage, and overhead—before you get into the black.

What's *good* about magazines is that you can pinpoint your market.

Men, boys, women, girls, psychology freaks, sexual deviates, motorcycle nuts . . . they all have their own little magazines. And some of the magazines can deliver combinations of these groups.

So when you've tested your ad in the newspapers (which is what I recommend) and you're ready to take a whack at the magazines, here are some tips:

Tip #1—Try to get a right-hand page. If your ad appears on a left-hand page, results will be drastically diminished.

Tip #2—Try to buy big enough space so you can be the only ad on the page. A full page insures it (in which case you want to request "editorial only" on the left-hand page). A two-thirds page in a "standard-size" magazine, if the other column is editorial, is a good buy. A *vertical* half-page in a "big size" magazine (like the Ladies Home Journal) will do the same job. I've bought a couple of *horizontal* half-pages—to my regret. People are conditioned to look first (and sometimes only) at the top of the page.

Tip #3—If you buy enough space, ask that there be "no backing coupon." Because if there's a competitive coupon on the "back" of yours—and it's cut out—you've lost a possible sale.

Tip #4—Ask if you can get a "free edit." Many magazines will give you one or more "edits" (small "articles" in their "Shoppers Guide Section") when you buy an ad. They won't produce a whole lot of orders (about the best I've done is $800), but every little bit helps. Other magazines, particularly the magazines directed at "Salesmen," may give you a good-sized article.

Incidentally, these "edits" can help you get started in business even if you have no money for advertising. Get a good 8x10 photo of your product at work, write a short, punchy ad—and send both out to all the magazines that have "Shoppers Guide Sections." If your product's new and exciting, quite a few may print it—and you'll be on your way! Dozens of magazines have these "Sections." If you want to know which they are, visit a newsstand, pick out the magazines that would appeal to your prospects, and look for it in the "Mail Order Section." The magazine's address will be there or, if not, somewhere in the first few pages of the magazine.

Tip #5—Base your advertising buying on *circulation*, not "readership." The "readership" will usually be three to four times as high as the circulation, and small circulation magazines often quote that figure because it's so much more impressive. But your $2 per thousand "rule of thumb" is based on circulation.

Tip #6—Another thing to check is "newsstand sales" as opposed to "subscriptions." (That information should be given to you along with a rate card.) For the Direct Response Business, a high percentage of newsstand sales is desirable. It means the purchaser of the magazine went to a little trouble to get it—and may read it more thoroughly.

Tip #7—Have you formed your own advertising agency yet?

When you're ready to get started on your magazine advertising, here's a partial list of people you can write to. Between them, they represent most of the magazines now being published. If you'll tell them what you're selling (preferably enclosing a copy of the ad), they should be able to suggest which of the magazines they represent might be suitable—or recommend a competitor.

They're in alphabetical order, and no endorsement is intended or implied. Some are personal friends. Others are friendly business acquaintances. A couple I just do business with—very carefully. But if you reread and study this chapter, you should be able to take care of yourself.

Campbell Reynolds
641 Lexington Avenue
New York, New York
(Irv Sperling)

David Geller Associates
8648 Wilshire Blvd.
Beverly Hills, California
(Alan Geller)

Mel Lenny Reps, Inc.
227 East 45 Street
New York, New York
(Mel Lenny)

Conde Nast Publications
3921 Wilshire Blvd.
Los Angeles, California
(Van Behal or Jerry Bronow)

Hammond Media Group
964 Third Avenue
New York New York
(Peter Hammond)

Lawrence Levine Assoc.
227 East 45 Street
New York, New York
(Ken Baratto or Dick Lindner)

Dane Advertising
7551 Melrose Avenue
Los Angeles, California
(Mildred Greene)

Brian Hayes Company
227 East 45 Street
New York New York
(Brian Hayes)

Newell, Snyder, Clarkson
225 Santa Monica Blvd.
Santa Monica, California
(Ted Clarkson)

Dauntless Publishing
111 N. La Cienega
Beverly Hills, California
(Lee O'Connell)

Ideal Publishing
295 Madison Avenue
New York, New York
(Larry Sandler)

Sanford Schwarz & Co.
16 West 46 Street
New York, New York
(Mort Tuller)

Dilo, Inc.
114 East 32nd Street
New York, New York
(Joe Sokol)

Kalish, Quigley, Rosen
Box 48838
Los Angeles, California
(Ann Gist)

Scott, Marshall, Sands
1830 West 8th Street
Los Angeles, California
(Jim Latta)

Direct Mail:

There's very little I can add here, because in terms of "how to buy it," it's a fairly simple medium. The only caution is to "shop" for printing prices because they can vary widely. And, of course, you can effect great savings by ordering large quantities. But don't step up your order until you've had a chance to test the "pull" of your letter.

Who do you mail your letters to? Well, what's the "profile" of your prospect? Man? Woman? Skiing enthusiast? Overweight? Earns $10,000 a year?

Mailing List Brokers have hundreds of lists and millions of names—and a lot of information about the people on those lists. You'll certainly want to contact them when you want to "rent" the names of the customers you've acquired. And if you want to do a mailing of your own, a conscientious Mailing List Broker can be a lot of help in "zero-ing in" on your target.

There are dozens of Mailing List Brokers listed in "Direct Marketing Magazine." I'm sure there are many other fine ones, but here are three I've done business with:

Dependable List, Inc.
257 Park Avenue South
New York, New York 10010
or
333 North Michigan   Florence Wolf, Inc.
Chicago, IL 60601   919 North Michigan Avenue
                                Chicago, IL 60611

Or you might check the Yellow Pages for someone nearby. You'll also find "Direct Marketing" for "Co-op Mailings." These are mailings made to specific groups (such as expectant mothers). You can participate with your particular offer (if it's pertinent) for a fraction of what it would cost you to make a mailing on your own.

Also, the Broker you select will be able to put you in touch with people in this business who, for about 2½ cents per piece, will include your advertising in their package or follow-up mailing. I heard about one large Direct-Selling luggage company who saved its business from bankruptcy using this advertising technique.

If the company you're piggy-backing with has customers who should be interested in your product, you'll probably do all right.

So now you know how to "think up" a product (and a product can be a thing or a service) . . . how to set your selling price and control your costs . . . you know the business procedures . . . how to write and produce your ad . . . and how to buy media.

Are you still too busy working for a living to make any money?

CHAPTER EIGHT

A GOOD IDEA DOESN'T TAKE MUCH MONEY!

The same gentleman who told me that "Most people are too busy trying to earn a living to make any money" gave me a business maxim I never forgot:

"A good idea doesn't take much money."

It's proved to be true for me. And I'll prove it can be true for you.

If you'll follow the principles I've outlined in this book, you're sure to come up with an Idea. At the very least, your Idea will double or triple your present income. Even if your Idea is nothing more than how to do what you're doing right now—better. Or even if it allows you to escape from your present job and take some other job you'll really enjoy.

But let's say that you come up with an Idea that has mass appeal—and you can—what then? Does it take a lot of money to make it a reality . . . to at least test its appeal?

No. It doesn't have to cost you a dime. Because when you come up with a really good idea, I'll be willing to buy it outright or pay you a royalty. You could make a lot of money, and I'll make more. But your only investment is a pencil and paper.

If you're able to put up some money, I'll be willing to be your partner. The percentage will depend on how much you're willing to risk, how much of the responsibility you're going to shoulder, and what you expect of me.

If you can put up all of the money and do most of the work, I'll be willing to contribute my peculiar talents and take a percentage of the profits.

So, as you can see, "a good idea doesn't take much money." You can spend a lot of money on a good idea, but that doesn't make it any better. And all the money in the world won't salvage a bad idea.

The beautiful part of a good idea is that it's self-financing. You can—and should—expand by plowing part of the profits back in. "Seed" or "venture" capitol should be small, something you can afford to lose. Not because, as every gambler says, "Desperate money doesn't win." Because desperate money does win—sometime. But you've reduced your odds for success.

I can think of a number of deals that I, literally, worried to death. Instead of going with my original concept, I kept changing it around, hoping to hedge my bet. I was playing a *destructive* game of "What would happen if—?" The ideas that I worked and reworked failed. No exceptions.

The ones I conceived in a white heat and pursued with enthusiasm succeeded about 50% of the time. That's a .500 batting average, and it's been enough to make me rich. Rich enough that when a friend I told you about (the one who made 11 million dollars in this business in eight years) jokingly asked me if I wanted a partner, I could honestly tell him, "No. I don't have any problems that money can solve." And you shouldn't want a partner either. Because you don't need one.

I told you before and I'll tell you again, "You can have everything in the world you really want." And you don't need to share it with me.

Nothing would give me more pleasure than to see you succeed on your own. And you will—if you do nothing more than apply what you're learning in these pages.

And, since you're still with me, maybe you will at least try it. I know it sounds "too easy." But it works! *Every* successful person uses some of these methods. The most successful use *more* of them. These successful people may not follow the form, but they surely follow the substance—because they couldn't succeed without it.

Dyna/Psyc is a *systematized* method for releasing creativity. All you have to do is follow the system. That's *all* you have to do. What have you got to lose?

I guess that two kinds of people will respond to that challenge. The first will be the person who's open-minded enough to admit that he's seen some evidence that the principle works—even in his own life—and the refinements we've offered might make it work *better*. The other kind of person is desperate, but not without hope. As one man wrote to me, "I'm a truck driver. I realize that the best I can get out of life right now is some overtime. There has to be something better than this." There is. I promise.

But I'm worried about all those people in-between. The ones who are saying "Oh yeah, all that Positive Thinking stuff. I know all about that." Oh no they don't! If they really knew—and put it into action—they wouldn't be in hum-drum jobs, or making "some" money, but not enough.

And what you have in your hands is not "just" Positive Thinking. I know. I took the Dale Carnegie course. I read Norman Vincent Peale and Napoleon Hill. And I got a lot out of them. But Dyna/Psyc takes over where Positive Thinking leaves off. Dyna/Psyc gives you everything that Science and Psychology have discovered about the System for Success.

Work the System—and the System will work for you!

Just the other night, I discussed Dyna/Psyc with a friend of mine. I've known him for 10 years. And for all of those 10 years (and all the years before, from what he tells me) he's been in financial hot water. He spends a good part of his time worrying about his bills, stalling creditors, cashing small checks at neighborhood stores so he can run to the bank and "cover" checks he wrote a couple days before. Time he could be spending making enough money to get rid of all those problems!

What a waste—because he's a brilliant man. Far too "intelligent" to believe that a few minutes a day practicing Dyna/Psyc could change his life. But he really doesn't *want* to change. He's "comfortable" in his misery. It's the way his life has always been.

When I talked to him about setting up some Daily Declarations and some Goals, he said, "I'm not really sure what I want. It really isn't important to me that I make a lot of money."

I said, "There's nothing wrong with not wanting a lot of money. But since you're apparently not willing to change your life style so you can get along on less, your goal should be to have *enough* money to live the way you are right now. I don't say that you 'should' have some new clothes and a new car. If you're happy with what you've got—fine. But if you want new clothes and a new car, make those goals, too—and include enough money to pay for them. The Chinese say that 'A man is rich who has enough.' Decide what's enough for you—and you've set your goals. But don't forget that *you're* going to have to change, too. If you can't make your own list of Intangibles, just work on all the ones I'll give you. All of us can use *some* improvement in *every* area."

The next time I talked to him, I asked him how he was coming—was he working on his Daily Declarations? He said "Kind of." I hope so, because that's better than nothing.

Can't you see how much pleasure I'd get out of his success—the knowledge that I had helped? Can you understand that if he fails, I've failed, too? Because I haven't found the right words. I haven't been able to get through. And that diminishes me.

Will you help me—by allowing me to help you? Will you at least try Dyna/Psyc? I can't do it for you. But I've shown you the way.

Maybe you're not interested in the Direct Response Business. I love it, because I think it's one of the last areas where a little guy can get a start, live where he pleases, work when he wants.

It may not be what *you* want. But you can't say that you "don't know how to go about it." Because you now know a lot more than I did when I got started—and maybe more than some of the people who are making a wad of money in this business right now.

And you can't say that you "don't have enough money" because you don't need *any*.

'I *recommend* that you try it on your own. But if, when you get your great idea, it's necessary or reassuring to get my help, I'll be glad to do it.

I don't really mind getting a share of the money you'll make. But if you keep it all, I'll be even richer!

Sincerely,

Joe Karbo